# TRAGEDY TO TRIUMPH
## Rebuilding a Traumatized Heart

# TRAGEDY TO TRIUMPH
## Rebuilding a Traumatized Heart

a memoir by
**Martha Bray**
with
Cheryl Stritzel McCarthy

Sidekick Press
Bellingham, Washington

Copyright © 2025 by Martha Bray

*Tragedy to Triumph: Rebuilding a Traumatized Heart*

All rights reserved. No part of this publication may be reproduced, distributed, or transmitted in any form or by any means, including photocopying, recording, digital scanning, or other electronic or mechanical methods, without the prior written permission of the publisher, except in the case of brief quotations embodied in critical reviews and certain other noncommercial uses permitted by copyright law. For permission requests, please address Sidekick Press.

Published 2025
Printed in the United States of America
ISBN: 978-1-958808-41-2
LCCN: 2025901889

Sidekick Press
2950 Newmarket Street, Suite 101-329
Bellingham, Washington 98226
sidekickpress.com

Cover design by Andrea Gabriel

# Contents

Prologue ... 1
Early Morning ... 3
Early Evening ... 7
Arriving Home ... 11
Not Just an Oopsie-Doopsie Accident ... 17
The Son Who Leads Us ... 21
The Best Business Fit in the History of Business Buyouts ... 25
Fast Forward to Disneyland ... 29
Just Don't Make a Mess When You Kill Me
   (It Would Upset the Children) ... 35
The First Christmas ... 41
Things I Know About Grief ... 47
The Most Important Dream ... 53
The Valentine's Day Store ... 59
Staying on the Sparkle Spectrum ... 63
Knocked off the Sparkle Spectrum ... 67
The Sentencing ... 71
I Can Scale Cliffs, I Can Leap Chasms ... 77
Take Me Out to the Ballgame ... 83
From Horror Movie to Rom-Com ... 87
Best Wishes, You Seem Like a Nice Person ... 91
The Washed-Up Cheerleaders and the Homecoming Queen ... 95
Here, There, Everywhere an Ax Murderer ... 99
The Best Day ... 103
The Kiss ... 107
Brain Chemistry and Other Mysteries ... 113
Is This *The Jerry Springer Show*? ... 119
He Is Kryptonite ... 123
Beauty and the Beast ... 129
I Will Come and Find You ... 135
Less Talking, More Doing, and True North ... 139
A Note from Martha ... 149
A Note from Cheryl ... 151
Bound for Glory by Cathy Pauley, friend of the Bray family ... 155
Grief Management Resources ... 157
Acknowledgments ... 159
About the Authors ... 161

# To Tyler and Tory:
# May the legacy continue.

Dad loved his work, he loved us, he believed in Jesus, and he hoped for heaven. Remember the Lou Holtz quote that your dad had taped to his bathroom mirror for thirty-plus years. His words were so simple and yet so profound:

Everybody needs four things in life:
Something to do
Someone to love
Something to believe in and
Something to hope for

Perseverance provides the bridge between suffering and hope.
(paraphrased from Romans 5: 3–5)

# Prologue

The first official report sounds so routine, so cold, so minimal: On Sept. 25, 2022, a sixty-four-year-old Bellingham man died as a result of a collision between two motorcycles on Highway 20 near Anacortes, Washington. Robert Bray was driving a motorcycle east on Highway 20 and continued through a green left turn arrow to go north on Bayview Edison Road. A thirty-year-old man from Snohomish, Washington, was driving his motorcycle west on Highway 20. He reportedly cut across lanes of traffic, ran a red light, and collided with Bray in the intersection.

Bray was pronounced dead at Island Hospital in Anacortes. The other man was airlifted to Harborview Medical Center in Seattle and has since recovered.

The reality is something else entirely. Leave aside, for a moment, the criminal backstory of the man who caused the collision. More on that later. My husband Bob's sudden traumatic death hit our world like a meteor slamming into Earth, changing everything, seeming to knock the very planet off course. In the two years since that dreadful day, everyone who knew Bob (and everyone is a lot of people, as evidenced by the seven hundred mourners who attended his memorial service) has asked us, over and over, how we are, how we're coping, how we're moving forward through the weeks and months of living hell following his death.

This book is my answer.

This book is also the written version of stories I've told verbally, stories that elicit goosebumps in those who hear them, stories that make eyes widen because truth is truly stranger than fiction, stories that make listeners exclaim, "You can't make this stuff up!" And I didn't. Everything in this book actually happened, though I've changed some names and identifying characteristics to protect privacy.

Some of the stories are what I call "God Winks," meaning events so insanely coincidental that divine intervention is the only plausible explanation. Lots of the stories are humorous, proving you can laugh in the face of disaster. And some of the stories may deliver comfort and solace to others reeling from profound grief. Perhaps my months of living a horror movie (with its startling and unexpectedly funny rom-com moments) could become a blessing for someone else.

As grief survivor Gary Sturgis says, "We are all just walking each other home."

I invite you, in these pages, to walk with me and our family and friends. Walk with me on this road I'm on, this road I would never have chosen, this road where everything is unfamiliar, and I have no idea what is just around the corner.

—Martha

Sunday, September 25, 2022

## Early Morning

I awaken to slivers of sunshine fingering their way around the shade covering the huge window of our second-floor bedroom. I luxuriate for a moment in our bed's comfortable depths, appreciating this room in this beautiful house that my husband Bob and I bought just a couple of months before. It's in a familiar neighborhood, though; I grew up in a house just down the road. Also nearby, across the lake near those towering fir trees, is the house where Bob and I lived for fifteen years, where we raised our two sons. From this bedroom window, we can see our old house, with its cheerful blue-and-white exterior paint that I chose years ago. Or we could if the shade was up. Which it's not, this early on a Sunday.

I stretch, feeling the comfort of soft sheets over a plush mattress, roll over, and see Bob lying close, still in pajamas but fully awake and grinning at me. His smile makes the lines on his tan face crinkle upward toward his newly graying temples. At sixty-four, Bob is still decently fit, though not quite as trim as he was on our wedding day thirty-eight years ago.

"It's going to be nice for the Oyster Run today!" he says.

He's so happy that I smile too. Bob's been looking forward to this ride all week. This week, like all his workdays as owner and hands-on manager of our wholesale dairy distributing business here in Bellingham, Washington, has required long hours, always-on people skills, and endless energy. As boss, the buck stops with him. But today, Sunday, he gets to ride his beloved Yamaha motorcycle with his friends on scenic roads through the Skagit Valley's fertile farmlands and picturesque little towns. They'll ride through autumn sunshine across acres of flatland delta laid down eons ago by the Skagit River as it flowed toward the Pacific Ocean. The small city of Anacortes is on Fidalgo Island, one of many islands off the coast of northwest Washington, but Fidalgo Island is linked by highway to the mainland. That makes Anacortes the perfect epicenter for the Oyster Run, the Pacific Northwest's largest motorcycle rally, with thousands of riders gathering today for live music, seafood, vendors, and good times.

Bob takes my face in his hands and kisses me before bounding out of bed. "It's been a long week slinging moo!" he says, stepping out of pajamas. He likes to call his livelihood "slinging moo." Dairy Distributing was founded in 1958; Bob bought it in 1992 from his dad and dad's partner. Since then, Bob has grown the business to more than two hundred accounts, with seven full-time employees and a fleet of trucks. It's a low-margin product line: milk, ice cream, eggs, cheeses, frozen treats, and such, delivered to customers that include schools, hospitals, nursing homes, and this area's seemingly endless coffee shops. Washington has fifty-seven coffee shops for every hundred thousand residents, more than twice as many as the national median. Bellingham itself has more drive-through espresso stands per capita than any other city in the United States.

As his father did, Bob knows his clients by name. "I was talking to Diane Brainard over at Old Town Café this week," Bob says, opening the closet to get his church clothes. We'll go to the 9:00 a.m. service at Northlake Community Church this morning, sitting in the same pew we always do, as we've done for years, before Bob goes out riding this afternoon. Bob pulls on dress pants and thrusts his arms into a button-down shirt.

"Diane's trying to retire too," Bob says, rummaging for his dress shoes on the closet floor. Diane, owner of Old Town Cafe, has been a customer for decades. "She said she's finding it hard to let go, as I am."

I smile into my pillow. So many of our business's customers are longtime friends. I know that if Old Town Café runs short of anything, all they have to do is call and Dairy Distributing will get over there quick with a case of eggs, milk, or cheese, Bob often delivering it himself. He likes to make the business's bank deposits himself too, in person every Monday, Wednesday, and Friday at People's Bank in downtown Bellingham, where the tellers know him.

I get out of bed and head toward my closet for my own going-to-church clothes, humming a hymn to myself, delighted that the day's weather looks perfect. Bob deserves a great ride today. He works hard, especially during the summer when the business sells a lot of ice cream. With the warm weather, plus a few employees out with Covid, he's been logging even more hours than usual. Added to that, he's been working to find a buyer for Dairy Distributing. That's a critically important and full-time job in and of itself.

After church and back home, we change clothes, Bob into motorcycle wear, me into a pickleball skirt. With Bob out riding, it will be the perfect afternoon for me to play pickleball with my besties, the treasured girlfriends I've had since middle school.

Bob and I have a quick lunch, making use of leftovers in the fridge, and I load our few dishes into the dishwasher. I'm standing at the kitchen window when Bob comes back in, geared up now for his ride, to give me a hug.

"Sunny and seventy-two!" Bob says, still grinning. "Perfect fall day for a ride."

I laugh a little because he's so happy that he's giving me a big kiss and extra-long hug before he goes to the garage to don his helmet.

His joy stays with me, filling me up as I stay at the kitchen window to watch him ride down our driveway, turn right, and then veer left as he departs our neighborhood.

That was the last time I saw him.

Sunday, September 25, 2022

## Early Evening

I see the bright yellow pickleball up high, within swinging range of my paddle. Woo-hoo! It's a high floater and I'm in perfect position at the kitchen line. I leap up and smack that plastic, perforated ball as hard as I can, right down the center of the opposite court.

"A clean winner! Martha, that's yours!" Across the net, my girlfriends Kim Bajema and Diane Marsh applaud the shot, even though they're rueful that they've lost the final game. My partner Shelly Beld and I high-five each other in victory.

It's been a great afternoon. We're at the Bender Fields public courts in Lynden, a little town fifteen miles north of Bellingham that's just south of the Canadian border. It's 6:30 p.m., so we four gather our gear, picking up a sweater here, a water-bottle there, gabbing nonstop before we head to our separate cars.

I drive my Toyota Highlander south from Lynden through farm fields and rural homes toward Bellingham, feeling lucky to have old friends like these. Shelly, Kim, Diane, and I have been friends since middle school. We were all cheerleaders at Sehome High School in Bellingham, graduating together in 1980. How many women get to hang with their besties from high school more than four decades after graduation? That thought makes me smile.

I'm at the intersection of the Hannegan Road and Sunset Drive in north Bellingham waiting at the red light, half listening to NPR on the car radio, when it strikes me: This was exactly where I was, exactly twenty-one years ago to the hour and the day, when the worst thing that had ever happened to me occurred.

I was thirty-nine then, married to Bob with two young sons. About 7:00 p.m. that evening of September 25, 2001, I was driving my Ford Windstar minivan with two other girlfriends along as passengers. I was stopped at the little rise of this intersection of Hannegan and Sunset at this same red light when a Honda Accord sped through the intersection and smashed into my minivan. An explosion of metal against metal, a sickening crunch, shattering glass, billowing smoke . . . would my gas tank explode into flames? We three women stumbled out of my crushed vehicle and saw before us what looked like a movie scene: two young men, having catapulted through their own windshield, lay atop the Accord's hood with lacerated heads, shards of glass embedded in their foreheads, and blood streaming down their faces.

Traffic backing up, a wail of sirens, ambulances, fire trucks. Police closing the road behind us. My minivan's front end separated from its passenger section, the front axle broken in half, the back window shattered. There was no fire; what we'd thought was smoke was an explosion of powder from activated airbags.

The two young men rolled off their hood and walked toward us, both weaving a little, not quite standing up straight. With slurred, halting speech, they asked if we were okay. It was quickly discerned that they were incredibly drunk, and thankfully, minimally injured. Neither had been wearing seatbelts. They were soon in the ambulance, handcuffed to the side rails. We three women were asked by first responders if we'd like an ambulance to the hospital. We declined. We weren't bleeding, had no bones broken, and three husbands on the way to rescue us. We were so stunned and grateful all of us were alive that I discounted the pain in my back and neck, later diagnosed as whiplash. (Years and decades later, after countless chiropractic treatments, massage therapy, and medical evaluations, neck pain from that whiplash still haunts me.)

My Ford Windstar was totaled. The drunk young men had minimal insurance. The financial consequences were crushing, too.

Twenty-one years later, driving alone across that intersection after this Sunday afternoon of pickleball as the memories of that awful evening flood through me, I feel a renewed realization that I could have died in my vehicle that night. The two drunks were doing forty miles per hour through that intersection when they hit my minivan. If they had hit my door instead of the engine, I would have lost at least my legs and possibly my life.

Heading toward home, I'm filled with thankfulness. Golden evening sunlight slants through the car windows and the radio is still on, but I barely hear it. My head, my entire being, is bursting with thanks to God that I have been able to watch my boys go all the way through middle school, high school, college, get married, and have their beautiful children. I had not died at thirty-nine that evening. Instead, I'd experienced so much joy, so much happiness, so much *life* with Bob and our sons, with family and friends, with our work and love and struggles and successes.

We were blessed indeed.

Sunday, September 25, 2022

# Arriving Home

I drive onto our winding street, the hymn I was humming early this morning running through my head again. I'm tired now, a little hungry, looking forward to getting home. But our house is dark. That's odd. Where's Bob?

I'm in the garage now, out of my Toyota Highlander. Bob's Yamaha motorcycle isn't in its regular garage parking spot. I go through into the kitchen, hanging my car keys on the hook. No lights on anywhere, no sound.

Then, out of the kitchen window, through the soft twilight of the autumn evening, I see a twin beam of headlights sweep across the lawn. A police car is turning into our driveway. What is happening? Why is our son Tyler being shoulder-carried up the driveway between two police officers? And there's Stephanie, our daughter-in-law, getting out of the cruiser, clutching the roof and door. She looks unable to walk. What? What?!

I fling open our front door, apprehension—no, terror—on my face.

"Mrs. Bray?" the officer says.

In an instant, I get the news. Bob died at the scene. Paramedics on the ambulance performed CPR for thirty minutes, reviving a pulse briefly but not his heart. His body is at the hospital in Anacortes.

In the time it takes an eye to blink, Bob is gone.

Shock and horror, disbelief, near-hyperventilating, a blur of words. A blur of faces, kind, compassionate faces belonging to first responders from Skagit County Sheriff and Bellingham Police Department, as well as someone from Support Officers of Whatcom County. We three family members, Tyler, Stephanie, and I, sobbing, hugging, collapsing on the nearby carpeted stairs leading up from our foyer. My heart seeming to stop. My breath coming in shallow, fast, between sobs. Keep breathing. Keep breathing. My brain thinking, "This is not happening. This cannot be happening."

"Mrs. Bray." Someone is speaking. "Mrs. Bray."

It's one of the officers. I see the deep blue uniform of the police officer, the dark brown uniform of the sheriff's officer. Their faces blur. Which one is speaking? Breathe, breathe.

He continues gently. "The most important task right now, and why we have a support officer here, is for you to notify all next of kin and anyone else who you deem should not hear this first on the news or via Facebook."

A task. From someplace outside my body, I understand I have work to do. I seem to be separated from my body, floating outside it, viewing the scene in the foyer, looking at all of us standing, sitting, moving, as if we're actors on a stage.

I look up, get up from the stairs, clutch the banister post.

The officer repeats, "This is why we have a support officer here, Brandi Morgan. She will help you make as many calls as you can, as quickly as you can. It was a big accident scene with lots of witnesses, and news coverage is already happening."

And so, the gut-wrenching calls begin. Brandi, who I soon understand is a trained volunteer with a local nonprofit officially named Support Officer Community Care, figuratively and sometimes literally holds my hand as I sort out the family tree and sequence of calls.

Of utmost importance is our son Tory, his wife Katie, and their two little ones, who live in a suburb of Seattle. All of them are at a cousin's wedding in Bend, Oregon. Stephanie gets through to Katie right away. It is the first call and the most devastating.

I call my sister-in-law Robin Bray in Port Orchard, Washington, a city west of Seattle. Her husband Mike, who is Bob's brother, is tasked with contacting Bob's sister Michelle and her husband Norm Dahl, who are traveling in Turkey and Greece.

We keep going. Tap the name, tell the news, cry; our anguished phone calls continue. Breathe, do what needs to be done. Think. Don't leave anyone out.

At some point during the evening, I learn why authorities contacted Tyler and Stephanie first; Tyler was listed as Bob's next of kin. Between calls, I glean their story: Two uniformed officers come to Tyler and Stephanie's front door. This catches the attention of their neighbor Rachel Frere, who astutely realizes nothing good is going to happen next. Rachel, who happens to be a teacher at the school attended by Tyler and Stephanie's kids Logan and Zoey, ages seven and five, comes over to shepherd the kids, taking them to the home of Stephanie's parents, Ben and Kimi Ebbeson, to spend the night. Tyler and Stephanie are instructed to pack an overnight bag and the officers drive them to our house.

Now more family members arrive in an erratic stream of devastation with tears, disbelief, hugs. Stephanie's brother Ryan and his wife Tessa Ebbesen; my sister Marlene and her husband Drew Thurston; my friend April Francis, who is a Bellingham police officer; and my uncle Bill DeHon from Mount Vernon, a little city south of us. Bill is a seasoned support officer like Brandi but for Skagit County, not Whatcom County where I live.

Calls and more calls. How am I managing to make these calls when I can't believe the words coming from my mouth? I tamp down my shock and horror and keep at it. I call my friend Arleen Watkinson and ask her to tell Doug and Sandy Thomas. I call my friend Sue Schwab and ask her to call our gang of six couples who live in Bellingham and also own houses in our Arizona community. I call our pastor from Northlake Community Church.

I'm ensconced on the couch in the living room, Brandi next to me, when more officers from the Skagit County Sheriff's office arrive with charging documents for me to sign, specifying that the collision that killed Bob was a vehicular homicide murder, not a vehicular homicide accident. Bob was riding safely, legally, following the green left-turn arrow when another motorcyclist ran a red light and hit him. The red-light runner has been helicoptered to Harborview Medical Center in Seattle with a broken nose and a nick in his carotid artery but is expected to live.

I sign the documents. Legally, I am the victim since Bob is dead.

Yet, the night does not end. At some point, I get a call from the organ donation company LifeNet Health, seeking permission to harvest Bob's corneas. (He'd registered as a donor long ago, then had forgotten about it.) Even through my fog of shock and devastation, I understand time is of the essence. I can't just say, hey, call me later, now is not a great time. And so ensues a surreal fifteen-minute conversation about Bob's health. Once again, I feel separate from my body, displaced from the scene in our living room. How am I reviewing the life of a man I kissed goodbye just hours earlier? Robotically, I answer every question. Repeatedly, the caller says what an important donation this will be. With Bob's corneas, someone who was blind will see.

I feel blinded myself. I wonder, gripping the phone with sweating palms, whether I will ever see, whether I will ever understand why this is happening.

Stephanie and Tyler eventually collapse into bed in the guest room. Dear Uncle Bill, who's returned after helping my sisters cope at their own homes nearby, beds down in the other upstairs bedroom. At 3:00 a.m., I land in my bed. I try not to see Bob's side, which looks as wide and empty as a snow-swept prairie. The bed, the room, the window . . . it is the same bed, same room, same house I'd left only hours earlier, but it is not at all the same and never will be again.

Monday, September 26, 2022

# Not Just an Oopsie-Doopsie Accident

I sleep, only to pop awake two hours later at 5:00 a.m.

Monday arrives with a vengeance. With a fresh jolt of shock, I realize the world is expecting to go on as usual. Employees will soon be on their way to our downtown building. Dairy Distributing's warehouses are full of perishable products. Clients who are responsible for restaurants and coffee shops and hospital dining rooms are expecting deliveries . . . goodness, the employees! I leap out of bed, my heart hammering. Are they to hear about their dead boss on the radio? What else haven't I thought of? Of what other urgent matters am I not even remotely aware?

I throw on clothes, swing into action. More phone calls, more friends and family, in and out. The doorbell rings, then rings again and again with flower deliveries from so many who are thinking of us, praying for us, wishing us well. A huge spread of sandwiches, fruit, desserts, and coffee is delivered. Soon the entire dining room table is covered with the well-wishes of friends and family, near and far. The scent of flowers and the aroma of coffee fill the room. Soon the whole family is here, all of us just trying to breathe, all of us starting to think about an appropriate service for this man we loved.

Time becomes a blur of tasks, tears, hugs. I'm told that the staff at Dairy Distributing is showing up at our building downtown, ready to work, telling each other, "That's what Bob would do."

Our son Tory and wife Katie arrive at the house, having left the wedding in Bend yesterday, immediately upon hearing the news. I hear their story: The ceremony was over, thankfully, with the reception getting into full swing, when Katie picked up Stephanie's call and heard the dreadful news. In a room loud with music and merrymaking, it was hard to hear, and even harder to believe. Tory looked at Katie, his smile changing to fear as he registered her expression, then to shock and disbelief. *This can't be right! My dad is so strong. Maybe he has a broken arm or something?* Katie shook her head. Tory's world stopped as he fell to the floor. Katie's parents took over, whisking them away, arranging flights to Bellingham. Tory and Katie's two children are still babies, really, and too young to understand.

This morning, Tyler and Stephanie's children are at school, with teachers instructed to shelter them from the news for one more day. After school, in the den with just the four of them, Tyler and Stephanie will tell their children. For Tyler and Stephanie, telling Logan and Zoey of the death of their adored PapaBob is one of the saddest moments of their lives.

I thought the shock and horror of Sunday evening couldn't get worse. Then it did.

We'd been told Bob had been hit in the intersection by another motorcyclist running a red light. But there is more, much more to the story. As we were to learn from public documents and news reports, investigators reported Michael E. Icenhour, thirty, of Snohomish, was riding in a "stupid and dangerous" way that Sunday afternoon, without regard for anyone's safety. Documents state that a State Patrol trooper witnessed Icenhour leading a group of motorcyclists while riding with only the back wheel of his motorcycle on the ground for about two hundred feet. When troopers tried to stop him, he accelerated into the intersection, ran a red light, switched directions at the last minute, and slammed into Bob.

There's more. *KOMO News* in Seattle reported that a year earlier, a Washington State Patrol helicopter video—that has since been seen thousands of times on YouTube—shows Icenhour driving recklessly, 104 miles per hour, on Interstate 405. When troopers finally caught up to him, they found illegal drugs in his backpack, but in 2021, the Washington State Supreme Court's "Blake Decision" had struck down drug possession as a felony. So Icenhour received a speeding ticket and was released, free to keep endangering others.

*KOMO News* would go on to quote our friend Ken Bell, a Bellingham port commissioner, to call on state lawmakers to revisit laws like the Blake Decision, as well as restrictions on police pursuits. "Quite frankly, I hold a lot of the state legislature responsible for the death of Bob Bray," Ken is quoted in the story.

There's more yet. King County court documents show that in 2013, Icenhour was convicted of robbery and gun theft during a burglary spree. He served six years in prison, and after he got out, Snohomish County prosecutors charged the thirty-year-old with raping a woman while she was sleeping. He posted bail on the second-degree rape charge.

We were to learn most of that history later. Today, Monday, Day One After the Horrendous Event, a group of us at the house are in the den viewing the authorities' online video of Icenhour's earlier race on Interstate 405 at 104 miles per hour. We see his recklessness; we see his face; we hear his excuses, his rationalizations. We see the cops find cocaine in his bag. It's all there, right in front of us on police cam. Then, we see him released.

The video sends us over the edge. Some in our group flee the room. Some dash for the bathroom, covering their mouths until they can retch into the toilet. Some stay put, steely-faced, and watch the whole thing, which is nearly forty-eight minutes long.

I don't retch or flee. I watch. I am numb.

Over the forty-five days until Icenhour's apprehension and the nine months until his plea bargain and sentencing, I was to learn this history is why the State Patrol officers sometimes had tears in their eyes as they interacted with, and cared for, our family. More than one let us know this case felt like one of their worst nightmares as well.

Tuesday, September 27, 2022

## The Son Who Leads Us

"It may be that one of you has something you want to say to the whole group," the grief counselor says, his eyes sweeping over the eighteen of us gathered in the living room.

Silence. No one says a word. It's Day Two, and we've arranged for a family therapist to come and try to teach us family members how to deal with tragedy.

Still no sound, other than a throat being cleared, a deep breath drawn in, a couple of derrieres shifting on the couch. Logan's on the couch, wedged between his mom and dad, his head covered with a blanket. Zoey's there too, quiet, hands clutched in her lap, her little face pale, eyes darting from face to face.

Randy, the therapist, is a slender, grandfatherly man on the plus side of sixty, with a welcoming expression and calm demeanor. He looks approachable. He looks like just what we need. I'm aware of his decades of experience dealing with those experiencing profound loss. Already this morning, he's explained that we would all likely be emotionally ricocheting among the five stages of grief for a long time; that there's no correct way to grieve; and that we'd often be at different stages from one another. I'm grateful that he's here. I had heard of the five stages of grief, first identified by Elisabeth Kubler-Ross in the late 1960s—denial, anger, bargaining, depression, acceptance—but never had a reason to pay attention to them. Before now. Now, we need to learn about grief.

He continues. "It may be that you have something to say but aren't sure how to say it." His voice is gentle with an undercurrent of strength.

Indeed. We've been bumbling around, no one knowing what to say, for forty-eight hours. We are walking zombies, each filled to the brim with swirling, boiling feelings that have no words.

Then my younger sister Marlene clears her throat. "I was driving today and came to an intersection with a green left-turn arrow, which was literally the last thing Bob saw before he was killed. I went into shock, couldn't breathe, had to pull over, couldn't stop crying. What am I going to do? Be unable to drive for the rest of my life?"

Randy looks at Marlene, but his words are for all of us. "After the shock of losing someone, random sights, sounds, and smells remind us of the one we've lost. Especially in the first months, these triggers come hard and fast." He stops, glances at our faces. We are all quiet, listening. "The grief feels overwhelming at first and some of the intense emotions that you feel today will return," Randy says. "But over time, triggered emotions occur less often and lose intensity. You can train yourself to respond positively to a trigger. As you're driving and see a green left-turn arrow, you can think, oh, how Bob loved riding on a beautiful day. It becomes a glimmer of his memory, a happy memory. Is this easy? No, it is not. It is exhausting. But you can choose to turn triggers into glimmers."

We look at him, doubt on our faces. Will we ever be able to do that?

"It's also okay to cry and be as sad as you need to be," Randy continues. "These normal emotions are part of the process of grieving."

More silence. Randy waits. I see he is comfortable with long pauses.

Logan takes the blanket off his head, looks at Randy. He's heard the invitation to speak from this kind-looking man at the front of the room, so he does. "I'm going to miss Papa because he played games with me," he says. He wiggles down off the couch, lays on the floor, and pulls the blanket over himself entirely.

It's no longer silent because some of us are now sniffling or sobbing outright.

Tyler takes a deep breath, stands. I look at him in surprise. Tyler, our firstborn, who's spent the last fifteen years working side by side with his dad at our World Headquarters of Dairy Distributing, has been sitting silent in the den for most of the last two days. Always a man of few words, lately he's hardly spoken at all.

In contrast to his usual neat demeanor, right now Tyler is unshaven, wearing loose basketball shorts and a polo shirt. His trademark sparkly, light-blue eyes are dull and rimmed with red. He pauses, takes another deep breath. "I need to say, I have forgiven the man who killed my dad."

My breath leaves in a whoosh. I think, *Yes, this is what we need to hear. This is what we need to do. Thank you, Tyler, for being the son who leads us. I have never been more proud to be your mom.* But all I can say is, "Thank you, Tyler. Thankyouthankyou," before hugging him, and then Stephanie, and Tory and Katie and everyone else who can cram into this hug that's growing larger by the second.

In the weeks to come, we will know what to say when anyone asks, "How are you doing? How's the family doing?"

"Okay," I will answer. "We are doing okay, because we know we will forgive the man who killed Bob."

This is the beginning of our path toward healing broken hearts. Forgiveness and grace. The most important things.

Wednesday, September 28, 2022

# The Best Business Fit in the History of Business Buyouts

Everyone at World Headquarters of Dairy Distributing in downtown Bellingham is pulling double duty to keep the place humming. Receivables are being received, deliveries are getting delivered. Hugs and tears are everywhere these first few days: at every delivery stop, with every line-haul semi-truck driver coming to the plant, with every businessperson who knew Bob—and they all did.

Today, Wednesday, for the first time, I do what Bob used to do almost every Monday, Wednesday, and Friday: go to Peoples Bank on the corner of Cornwall and Magnolia downtown and make deposits for Dairy Distributing. I pull open the glass doors and enter the modern brown-brick building and see four tellers at four windows. I see their faces lose their professional, smiling demeanor, their expressions change from pleasant greeting to deep sadness in an instant.

I look from one to the other, and soon we are all in tears, deep breathing, struggling to find words. They're trying to hold it together, in a bank-teller sort of way, but who are we fooling? We are all shocked and horrified and sad.

But I do not have to do all, or even most, or maybe any more of Bob's jobs, because the next day, what I began to call the "A-Team" showed up en masse on the front deck of my house: Ken Bell, commissioner at the Port of Bellingham; Doug Thomas, president and CEO of Bellingham Cold Storage; John Carter, recently retired chief financial officer for the Port of Everett; and Doug Forhan, retired business owner (and the guy who, with his wife Cara, introduced Bob and me in 1982). All longtime friends, all highly accomplished, each one an all-around genius. In the midst of my shock and grief, with my world knocked off its axis and Dairy Distributing suddenly without its leader, they stepped up. Doug Forhan took over Bob's cell phone and manned his desk. Doug Thomas, with his kindness and business intelligence, had essential repairs made to the cooler, among other tasks. Both helped the able team already in place at Dairy Distributing (including general manager Steve Swanson, who is Bob's cousin, and our son Tyler, who's worked there for years) with the unexpected extra workload. Ken Bell, tapping a deep well of creative thinking and resourcefulness, would soon find and land a buyer for the business. John Carter would oversee the accounting that would accompany the buyout. It was to be an overwhelming amount of work, about which I knew almost nothing.

The next few days pass in another blur of tasks and tears. For me, most urgent is creating a celebration of life for Bob, an event I expect several hundred people will attend. (Afterward, there will be a reception at another venue, and I remain grateful for the tremendous work done on this after-event by friends Sandy Thomas and Danielle Larson, who handled the caterer, venue, alcohol license, tables, chairs, tablecloths, centerpieces, and more.)

On Day Eight After the Horrendous Event, I am also grateful to Ken Bell when he and two men from Troia Foods, a family-owned business headquartered in Monterey, California, meet me on my front deck to talk business buyouts. John Troia, CEO, and George Logan, chairman, have flown up in a private plane; our friends Danielle and Tony Larson of Whatcom Business Alliance, an organization that supports local business, met them at the Bellingham airport and drove them to my house.

Within a few days, I held in my hands Troia Foods' letter of intent, which met every one of my requests, including hiring all the employees. It felt, and would turn out to be, a match made in Heaven—perhaps literally. They treated everyone with such grace and kindness. I felt they understood our trauma fog, our sudden and wrenching bereavement, on a deep level.

As I would learn six months later—in a hotel at Disneyland, of all places—they did understand, in a way no other business suitor could.

Early March 2023

# Fast Forward to Disneyland

"Closer, stand closer together," urges the woman holding my phone, wanting us to all fit in the photo she's taking at my request. Our group—me, Tory and Katie with their two little ones, Tyler and Stephanie with kids Logan and Zoey, plus my sister Marlene—obligingly cram closer together beneath the iconic entrance sign proclaiming, "Disneyland, The Happiest Place On Earth."

Bob and I had planned this trip to Disneyland for our kids and grandkids months ago. We'd spent time happily anticipating the fun of having everyone together, imagining the children's delight, their parents' smiles. I'm grateful to Marlene for stepping into Bob's place, and I depend on her support, but in this moment, as we all shift closer for our photo, Bob's absence feels like a wound freshly torn open. I take a deep breath to steady myself. Beyond the sign, which is jauntily topped with a metal cutout of the classic Disney castle and blue, pink, and yellow metal banners, we see the green fronds of towering palm trees wave in the breeze under a perfect blue sky. It's perfect weather for our perfect day at the perfect family park.

"Everybody say cheese!" The woman, a stranger who's agreed on the spot to take our photo, taps the button a second time, then a third. "Three tries, one of them should have everybody's eyes open," she says, handing the phone back to me. "A perfect family photo! Enjoy your . . ." But she stops short, because at that moment, at the happiest place on Earth, I, along with most of my family members, burst into tears.

"I'm sorry, I'm sorry," the woman blurts, confused, and flees ahead of us into the park.

I can't explain to her or anyone else how latent grief sometimes rears up and smacks you like a wave on the beach, a mighty wave that sneaks up from behind, a wave that you never see coming.

After settling into the Grand Californian Hotel—the trip is a splurge for family, after all—I pass a hotel employee whose nametag says "Fred, from Monterey, California."

"Monterey?" I ask, intrigued.

Pushing a room-service wheeled cart topped with covered dishes and iced glasses, he pauses and nods, giving me the standard employee's "you're-the-customer" smile.

"You're from Monterey!" I say, delighted. "Do you know the Troia Foods family?"

Did he! He warms up and tells his story. He'd arrived in Monterey decades ago as an immigrant, barely speaking English, constantly hungry, desperate for work. Troia Foods fed him, helped him, hired him. He would never forget their kindness. "But in the early '70s, something terrible happened, and all Monterey was sad," Fred says.

My brow wrinkles with a question, but just then another hotel-room door opens, a woman looks at Fred, inquires "Room service?" and Fred with his cart scurries away.

I would discover the answer to my question two weeks later and more than a thousand miles away, back in Whatcom County at the Whatcom Business Alliance Awards Black & Gold Gala.

March 23, 2023

The ballroom at the deluxe Semiahmoo Resort, situated some thirty miles north of Bellingham on a beautiful spit of land that juts into the sea, glitters with gold décor gracing the stage and dining tables. Women wear sequined cocktail attire or long gowns, men are in suits and ties, some in tuxedos. The annual Black & Gold Gala honors local businesses, but this year, Troia Foods' owners and managers have flown in to join tonight's festivities, since Bob is being posthumously honored with the coveted Lifetime Achievement Award.

That's not the only award being given tonight. Other annual awards open the festivities to honor small business, public service, Businessperson of the Year, Employee of the Year, and Start-up of the Year. I'm particularly pleased when Start-up of the Year is awarded to Craig Cooper and Courtney Jenkins, fellow pickleball players, for their launch of Armory Pickleball. They started an indoor site for the game I love within an old, unused, castle-like building in Bellingham. The applause that greets their award is well-earned.

Then to the last, the Lifetime Achievement Award. The chatter from four hundred guests stills as Doug Thomas, president and CEO of Bellingham Cold Storage, takes the stage to speak about how Bob ran his business with dedication, with heart, and with trust in employees and customers. Doug not only lists Bob's business achievements but shares memories of Bob as his friend, the two of them fishing for salmon together, boating and shrimping, telling jokes, going to Cougars' games at their alma mater,

Washington State University in Pullman, Washington, with Bob loyal to the crimson and gray even when the team "Coug'ed it."

Ken Bell takes the stage, speaking of his decades-long friendship with Bob, about sharing breakfast on Friday mornings at Arlis's Restaurant on Cornwall Avenue downtown, about how he and Bob would help each other with anything, of the near-miraculous arrangements that resulted in Troia Foods buying Bob's business after his death.

"You couldn't have asked for a better partner," Ken says. "Troia Foods stepped into that role and became a part of us, part of the fabric of Bellingham. When you look at the way this buyout came together, there's no way you can't see God's hand in this. There's no way anyone could've orchestrated this, all the events that came together to make it happen."

With each speech, each accolade, our family struggles to keep tears at bay. Sometimes it's the kindest words that can unleash a torrent. In my seat at my table, I marshal all the strength I can muster to hold it together, to smile and nod my thanks. Breathe, breathe. Do not cry.

Tyler and Tory take the stage to receive Bob's award on his behalf, and four hundred people, with understanding and respect for this moment, stand and somberly applaud.

After all the speeches and awards, over the clatter of dishes as waitstaff begin to clear tables, Tyler, who works for Troia Foods now, seeks out CEO John Troia to say hello. Tyler asks about the incident in the early 1970s that shook all of Monterey.

John tells Tyler the story. When John was eighteen, his uncle, who owned Troia Foods then, was shot in the face by a heroin addict in the company parking lot over a two-thousand-dollar bank deposit his uncle was carrying.

And just like that, in the blink of an eye, they lost their family member, their CEO, their leader. They know what it's like.

What are the chances of me encountering Fred the waiter in that hotel corridor in Anaheim? What are the chances of that same waiter having worked, decades ago, for Troia Foods in Monterey? What are the chances of me mentioning that to Tyler, of Tyler asking John, of John telling of a tragedy that happened decades ago, a tragedy that made this company uniquely able to understand us?

Ken Bell had said it was impossible to not see the hand of God in this, but Ken was speaking only of the many and unusual machinations that brought him to Troia and Troia to us. But Ken didn't know he'd found possibly the only family-owned food company in the world that would understand us on this level. What are the chances?

This is what I call a "God Wink," meaning an event so insanely coincidental that divine intervention is the most plausible explanation.

As I would begin to say more and more frequently as the weeks and months rolled by after the Horrendous Event, you can't make this stuff up.

Back to December 2022

## Just Don't Make a Mess When You Kill Me (It Would Upset the Children)

Before the God Winks at the business awards banquet in March 2023, in early December 2022, I fled the state. I left our home in Washington for my home in Arizona, literally thinking of never coming back.

During those first weeks after Bob's death, being alone in our home in Bellingham had become unbearable. A warrant had been issued for Bob's killer, but he was still on the loose, likely nearby, and thoughts of him and what he might do populated my waking and sleeping hours. Traumatic grief became a strange animal that romped through my mind, refusing to behave, trampling any good thoughts, bent on delivering fear and disorientation. Some mornings I would awaken hoping the nightmare was over, but, nope, it was always a new day to try to keep breathing through the wreckage, to summon the effort to keep moving forward with my shattered heart.

Along with all that came thoughts of suicide. During those early weeks, I did not care whether I lived another day. That is how much pain traumatic grief delivers.

However, the thought of never returning to Bellingham was irrational. Most of my extended family lives in Washington, including all my grandchildren. My family, sons and daughters-in-law, and siblings and cousins . . . goodness, Christmas is coming, and I am still the owner of the big family home where we all typically gather for the holiday, feasting, playing cribbage, having nerf-gun fights in the dark.

I get on a plane and fly to Bellingham International Airport, which is conveniently close to Costco, where I stop and load up on food. I would have grandchildren Logan and Zoey, newly off school for the extended Christmas break, at my house tomorrow.

I pull up to my big, dark, lonely house about 9:00 p.m., unload the car, and collapse into bed. I was just falling into an uneasy sleep when I heard him. An intruder. An intruder downstairs, banging around my kitchen. Crash! Shatter! Something glass smashed against the hard tile floor.

A normal person would have leapt up, heart in her throat, clutching bedsheets to her chest, thinking "911," thinking of her phone far away, plugged in on the kitchen counter. A normal person might have screamed to warn him off, to let him know that this house that looks deserted is not. A normal person might have hidden in a closet, heart thumping, hoping he'd find a valuable or two downstairs and be off.

But I am not normal. I am in a chronic state of traumatic grief, and I do not care whether he kills me or not.

Clatter, bang! I hear more items hit the floor. Hangers from a closet? What *is* that? I stay in bed. I'm oddly calm. I don't care.

In fact, this intruder might be helpful. I think, *please just kill me in my bed and don't make a mess, as I don't want to upset the children.*

Eventually, the noises stop. I go back to sleep.

In the morning, as I rush out to drive to Tyler and Stephanie's place to pick up Logan and Zoey, the house doesn't look too bad, just a few things askew. We three arrive back at the big house and come in from the garage to find more shattered glass on the kitchen floor. Dang intruder! I vacuum it up. I walk calmly through the house. Are we safe? More to the point, are these precious children safe here? I walk through the kitchen, the dining room, the living room, the den.

Then I see him, perched on the back of the recliner in the den. He is a twelve-inch-tall raven. I draw in a quick breath of surprise. I see a streak of white guano dribbling down the fabric upholstery of the recliner. I see a black feather on the floor, another on the windowsill. I see the raven cock his head at me. I see his black beak, his beady black eye sizing me up . . .

"A bird! A bird!" Logan and Zoey yell in unison, and the raven takes off, flying at the ceiling, flapping against the light fixture.

"Whoa! A bird in the house!" Logan is leaping up and down like a bobber on the end of a fishing pole.

"A bird, a big bird!" Zoey is running for the den door. "Nana, catch it!"

But the raven has other ideas. He bangs against the den window, falls to the carpet, flies up again, swoops around the light fixture, flies up and down and out through the den door. The kids jump and whoop, half excited and half scared but fully vocal.

I'm thinking fast. "Okay, Logan, Zoey, we'll close all the blinds in the house," I say. "We'll make the house dark. Logan, open the front door, wide, and leave it open. The bird will fly toward the light from the front door. Zoey, come with me. I need your help to close blinds and drapes."

We three sprint around the house, upstairs, downstairs, dodging the raven who is madly flying into walls, kitchen cabinets, closed doors. I see a blob of guano on the white carpet of the living room, another streaking the back of a kitchen chair. Feathers lie here and there on the hallway floor, the kitchen counter. From the foyer, the raven flies up the open stairs leaving small puffs of black down floating in the air. I dash up the stairs after him into the bedrooms, drawing drapes, dropping blinds as fast as I can.

I head back down to see Logan in the foyer below, popping up and down with excitement. "What about that window, Nana?" In the two-story foyer, Logan points to the arched window above the front door. "There's no shade on that one!"

And that is the window the raven is flying into, over and over, ignoring the wide-open front door beneath it. Then the bird's away again, darting down the hallway, into the kitchen, with Logan right behind it. Logan yells, "Watch out for the poop!" just before his foot, his bare foot, lands on an errant piece of shattered glass.

I dash into the kitchen a microsecond too late and see bright red blood seeping from his toe. Logan is trembling, scared by the amount of blood, trying not to cry, almost succeeding. "Logan, Logan," I say, gathering him into my arms. "We'll clean that up and take a look at it." We head into the powder room, Zoey trailing us, the raven perching for a moment on a chair back, cocking his head as if he's also interested in the bloody foot.

I clean and bandage Logan's foot. The cut is not deep, notwithstanding the amount of blood. The raven flies back into the foyer and out the front door. I shut the front door, put Logan and

Zoey on the couch in the den with a couple of books. I change into hazmat gear, otherwise known as old jeans and a paint-spattered shirt, and spend the next thirty minutes mopping up blood, poop, feathers.

The Three Stooges' skit, featuring Logan, Zoey, and Nana, with guest star The Raven, is officially over. It had a good run but the curtain's come down on it. Literally.

December 2022

## The First Christmas

After the Three Stooges' skit featuring the raven intruder, our family faced a daunting hurdle: our first Christmas without Bob.

When people say "the first Christmas," they usually mean the one in the stable in Bethlehem. But to us, with our world knocked sideways, the first Christmas was looming ahead. We couldn't ignore it; the day would arrive whether we wanted it to or not. And we were in no position to celebrate.

To gird myself for Christmas without Bob, I'd already attended an in-person, free class called "Surviving the Holidays" offered by GriefShare, a national program with support groups. I'd gleaned many tips among a consensus that yes, this would be hard. Connecting with other grievers was helpful; I would not be the only one to feel the difficulty of celebrating huge, once-joyful holidays now highlighted by loss and sadness. (You can find resources, including GriefShare, in the bibliography of this book.)

As the days in December marched inexorably toward the twenty-fifth, my ever-present grief acquired a new overcoat of bleakness tinged with panic. Holiday lights, giftwrap and ribbon, and an endless loop of Christmas music were everywhere. Wasn't the immense weight of everyday grief enough? Did it have to have the holidays on top to make it worse?

Thank goodness for children, especially our littles, who unwittingly arrested this downward spiral.

*Ding-dong!* Our doorbell chimes, then rings again and again, reverberating through the house. In the days before Christmas 2022, I open our front door to welcome family members who swirl into our foyer, propelled by fierce winds, blitzing snow, and lashings of freezing rain. Western Washington is experiencing something called an "atmospheric river," which keeps socking it to us with powerful winds, extreme cold, and heavy snowfall. (My dear neighbors had cleared deep snow from our steep driveway a few days prior.) Now, some Whatcom County roads are closed due to flooding, downed power lines and trees seem to be everywhere, Bellingham's airport is closed due to ice-glazed runways, and the levee on the Nooksack River will soon breach. With storm after storm slamming the entire Pacific Northwest, Washington's governor will later declare a state of emergency,

Extended family, bless them, show up despite conditions; the whole Bray family trudges across the state to be together on this first Christmas. A niece and a nephew and his wife arrive with stories of their harrowing, snow-whipped drive from Moscow, Idaho, which has taken eleven hours instead of the usual seven. Bob's brother Mike and his wife Robin drive through the snowy deluge from their home in Port Orchard on the Kitsap Peninsula in Puget Sound; Tory and Katie with their two little ones come from their Seattle suburb, as do a nephew and his wife with their two; Bob's sister Michelle and her husband Norm with their son Evan come from across town; Tyler and Stephanie with children Logan and Zoey come from their home five minutes away from ours.

Amid hugs and greetings peppered with travel stories, I feel afresh the searing pain of Bob's absence. Somehow, at unexpected moments, I half-expect him to be in the kitchen, sharing a beer with a son, the two of them leaning against the kitchen counter laughing at some shared joke. Somehow, for a microsecond, I think he'll come in from the garage any minute now with his winsome smile and a joy-filled hug for our grandkids. Why does my traumatized human mind trick me like this?

As the foyer fills with the chatter of grandkids, with dropped wet boots and thick-lined winter coats, I see with a stab of clarity that everything is the same, and everything is different.

Bob and I had hosted the family Christmas for eighteen years. For every one of those years, decorating the tree before the holiday had been a welcome task. Against a soundtrack of Christmas music, I'd unpack ornaments which only looked like trinkets but were really memories in tangible form.

This year, decorating had required a herculean emotional effort, but it got done, and now, as family members arrive, our house looks festive as always. On our tree, I see the treasured ornaments from places Bob and I traveled: the palm tree from Maui, the tiny Eiffel Tower, the miniature French chateaux. I see the darling ornaments made by the kids at Bellingham Christian School, the German ornaments from the Bavarian-like mountain town of Leavenworth in central Washington, the bat-and-ball ornament from the Baseball Hall of Fame in Cooperstown, New York. It's the same, but I am different. Would I ever feel like buying an ornament again? Oh, the memories in those tissue-lined, compartmentalized cardboard boxes! Memories of the life we lived together . . . that is no more.

But now, with all extended the family finally here, we put on a happy face and do normal things, as normal as we can muster. We play UNO with the kids, cribbage with the adults. Everything is the same—I lose against Logan and Zoey in UNO—but everything is different.

On Christmas Eve before the kids' bedtime, we gather in the living room around the fireplace, lights dim, everyone snuggled in comfy seats. Outside, snow mixed with freezing rain batters against windows and streetlights illuminate tree branches tossed skyward by the wind. Bob's brother Mike, settled in an easy chair near the fire, is reading Luke 2:1-20 for us this year. "And it came to pass in those days, that there went out a decree from Caesar Augustus, that all the world should be taxed . . ." The familiar words wash over me like a gentle slosh of a warm bath, like a benediction from Heaven. Everything sounds the same, but everything is different. Breathe, breathe, try to be normal, choose to be happy. I see flickering firelight on the faces gathered around, each so dear. Logan and Zoey, silent now, watch Mike with shining eyes. Tory is deep in an armchair with his tiny, snoozy toddler on his lap; Katie cuddles the baby. Oh, where is Bob? Why isn't he here? Why did it have to happen?

Mike's voice resonates deep, steady. "And she brought forth her firstborn son, and wrapped him in swaddling clothes, and laid him in a manger, because there was no room for them in the inn."

On Christmas Day, everything is the same, and everything is different. As always, Christmas music from the sound system rings through the house. One song especially makes my throat catch, country singer Scotty McCreery's "Christmas in Heaven." The lyrics seem written for us as the singer wishes for a loved one's return and wonders what Christmas in Heaven is like. But the music fades into background noise as kids open gifts in a flurry of joy and adults nod their thanks. The house fills with the familiar aroma of roasting turkey, of sage-and-parsley stuffing made moist with broth and butter. The meal is prepared mostly not by me, which makes me smile.

During dinner, we act normal, talking, smiling, eating. Everything is the same, and everything is different. Afterward, we sit around the table, bellies comfortably full, dishes still in front of us, my daughters-in-law pouring hot tea and coffee, when Zoey pipes up.

"I bet PapaBob is having a really good day in Heaven," she says.

I look up, pause, my cup of tea suspended halfway up from the tabletop. Steam curls up from my fragrant drink. I am familiar with Zoey's emotional intelligence, yet I'm still stopped short when I hear it.

"I bet PapaBob is with Shea the dog," Zoey says, forking into the wedge of apple pie on a dessert plate before her. She takes a bite, talks with her mouth full. "I bet there's a really big birthday cake for Jesus."

So sweet. So precious. I put down my cup, smile at her, at all of them, and quickly exit the dining room. I need to wrap my head around this and allow myself to cry just a bit. As I did yesterday, I force myself to feel thankful. Alone in the den, I take a moment to pray that when I die, the tragedy of Bob's murder will make sense. Right now, it does not make sense. Not at all.

I think of the Bible reading from last night: "And the angel said unto them, fear not, for behold, I bring you good tidings of great joy . . ." A child, the light of the world. Now my own precious little ones, all of them spilling over with joy at Christmas, all of them helping us choose to be thankful, Zoey helping us choose an eternal perspective instead of an earthbound one.

All of them helping me choose to remember that Heaven is real, and Bob is there. And he is really fine. There is a really big cake. And he loves cake. But more important, he loves Jesus.

In the days after Christmas, I gain clarity as to why we work so hard to impart spiritual truth to the young children in our lives. We need them to say the truth back to us, to make it even more real, to bolster our understanding of eternity. My little ones, my transparent little ones, say authentic truths, truths I need to hear. The same thing, if said by an adult, would land differently. When it comes from little ones with no filters, the truth can land perfectly. Love those littles!

Weeks and Months
After the Horrendous Event

# Things I Know About Grief

We were all just rolling through life, doing our jobs, raising families, working hard, loving our people, going to church—then *bam!* We now need to know about grief.

We literally knew nothing, because our lives to this point had been mostly grief-free. Sure, we'd lost a dog or two, and three of our four wonderful parents had passed away in their eighties or nineties. We miss them. But that grief felt normal and natural. There was no shock and horror at circumstances surrounding their deaths.

Here is what I now know for sure about grief. Here is what has helped me from the early weeks through the two years following Bob's death.

Embrace the many kindnesses of people who show up. Friends, neighbors, business colleagues, people I have not seen for years. They feel this with us. They want it to be better. I have received oh-so-many hugs! Long hugs from people who just want us to feel better. Nobody knows what to say. There are no words. But the hug says it all. The hug says I'm standing with you. It says, I see you. It says, I know this is hard. It says, I want it to be better.

It is as if some power from their hearts can flow into yours. It is as if they can give you solace that might result in even an ounce of healing. That is what they want. That is what I want. (If you are a single man and you know the widow, just give her a side-arm hug. Otherwise, it is going to look and feel weird.)

Then there are the books, those handy little packages of wisdom created by those who've taken this trip before, this trip none of us would have chosen. (I've listed books plus other resources in the Bibliography.) My favorites include *Option B: Facing Adversity, Building Resilience, and Finding Joy*, co-authored by Sheryl Sandberg, the former COO of Facebook, after the sudden death of her husband. This book was given to me on Day Two After the Horrendous Event by my neighbors across the street, a widow and widower who found each other.

Option B is a great concept: We no longer get to live our Option A, our first choice, so . . . on to Option B.

Option A, which most of us never think about because we're busy living it, means you and the love of your life live together before dying simultaneously at an advanced age. That option has vanished. For me, it evaporated in a shattering explosion of a motorcycle rider evading the law, crashing into my safe-riding husband.

"Gone," as I said.

So . . . let's pull ourselves together and rock Option B. Go on a trip, do all the fun things you've thought about, do the best you can while knowing that everyone knows you really wanted Option A. But darn it. You are going to *rock* Option B. That is what I decided to do. That is what Bob would want for me. He doesn't want me to sit here and cry and die a thousand deaths missing him.

The interesting thing is, when your friends know you're trying to rock Option B, they want to do that too. (Set aside for a moment the hard fact that almost everyone I knew who was anywhere near my age was married. I was acquainted with just one widow whose husband had died of Covid complications three months before.) Never mind the obstacles; whatever the circumstances, we will make it work. Let's go hot air ballooning during sunrise in Arizona; a quick Google search shows several choices near my home there. Let's go on a cruise to Italy, Greece, and Turkey and play pickleball on the top deck of the cruise ship. Let's reclaim the date of September twenty-fifth, the day Bob died, and spend the first-year anniversary of the death traveling with friends and family in Branson, Missouri, doing things we have never done before, seeing things we have never seen before. Let's go on a horseback ride at sunset through the San Tan Mountains near my Arizona home. Let's do this! Let's rock Option B, because that is the option we have now.

You should know that all of this took time. I had to learn to allow myself to "feel the feels," as I call it, to walk through my grief, to not stuff my feelings down deep. I had to feel them. And feel them again. What I know now is, you will eventually be okay. I learned that the more new and happy memories I made, the better I felt. Life does not have to be horrible and sad forever. Option B can be almost as good as Option A, something I would never have believed in the early months. But we have to choose it.

Another favorite helpful book is *It's OK that You're Not OK* by Megan Devine, who witnessed the accidental drowning death of her beloved partner Matt. She understands traumatic grief. She understands our culture of anti-grief, our culture that treats grief as a disease to be cured, a problem to be solved. That's part of the reason grief is so hard. It is foreign to us. Grief is going to touch us all at some point. She writes, "Grief is simply love in its most wild and painful form. It is a natural and sane response to loss."

A favorite resource for me is anything by Gary Sturgis, a grief survivor who does speaking tours, blogs online, and wrote *Surviving: Finding Your Way from Grief to Healing*. He became a widower in his early fifties. He speaks of coping and walking and doing our best, acknowledging that this is *hard*. But we're doing it. He is like a cheerleader for grievers. He gets us. He is us. My favorite quote from him remains, "We are all just walking each other home."

I also recommend the 2023 documentary/drama *After Death*, in which scientists, authors, and near-death survivors explore mortality and the afterlife.

One of the valuable things I know about grief came from my pickleball-playing friend Ted, who had lost his twenty-two-year-old daughter in a horrific accident about five years earlier. One day after our game in the Armory building in Bellingham, Ted said he was thankful for the way traumatic grief had expanded his heart and mind, thankful that his mind thinks in new ways, thankful that his heart can hear and feel others' grief. His own grief resulted in true compassion, a word that literally means to suffer together. That process, Ted said that day, can't happen any other way.

And of course, I recommend you read your Bible. God loves you and has many things to teach you. If you choose to hold onto faith, choose to believe God is sovereign, it can become your cornerstone of good thoughts. Yes, bad things happen, and we don't immediately see any good that might come of it. Remember the well-known story of life as a tapestry where we see only the ugly, confusing back side, with knots and hanging threads forming a baffling, random mess. But God is still working on the tapestry. He is making something beautiful. We just can't see the other side yet. Someday, we will.

What I know about grief is that we have to choose to be happy, choose to find all the little things for which to be thankful.

Each trigger of grief, though painful and difficult at first, can eventually become a glimmer of something good, a reminder of a happy memory. See the trigger and choose to turn it into a glimmer of good. Choose how you'll frame it in your mind.

You will begin to see life in new ways.

Four Months After the Horrendous Event

## The Most Important Dream

My rocking chair creaks rhythmically, back and forth, back and forth, as moonlight streams through the huge window of our second-floor bedroom. The view from our bedroom—my bedroom now—overlooks the northern tip of Bellingham's freshwater Lake Whatcom. Its long expanse shines silver in the dark. High up in a fir tree by the shore, an owl hoots, its slow "hoo-hoo" echoing the creak of my rocker.

It's after midnight. The first Christmas without Bob has come and gone. All the family, near and far, have departed for their homes, jobs, school. I am alone, holding the deep green velvet-wrapped metal container of Bob's ashes in my lap, staring unseeing out the window. Off to the right across Lake Whatcom is our previous home, right on the water where Bob and I lived for fifteen years, where we raised our sons. The boys were in high school, then at Wenatchee Valley College and Whitworth University during those years. My mind drifts back to that house, to the gatherings of friends, the boating, the barbecues on the deck. The stand-up paddleboard with Tyler's labs, Shea or Hunter, riding shotgun out front. Leaping off the dock and swimming through sun-spangled water to our little inflatable "island."

Our boys became men, moved out, married. Bob and I sold the lakeside home and bought another twenty-five miles to the north in the ocean beach town of Birch Bay. That was fine until the pandemic, which delivered a lonely two years of Covid-era living at what felt like the edge of the known world. Enough of that! We upped sticks and moved again, back to the familiar Lake Whatcom neighborhood, and bought this house on a hill with an expansive view, with four thousand square feet of living space so the whole family could come visit any time they wanted. This huge house is where I hosted the Christmas just past. It's where I am now, rocking, cradling that container of ashes, thinking. We bought this house a mere seventy days before Bob died.

The rocker creaks, the owl hoots, but I hear neither. I am forcing my mind to choose to be thankful that I'm in this house now. I would not have been able to live in the lakeside house without Bob, because I would've kept looking for him to come walking in from the garage every evening around 5:00 p.m. That is what life was like for a solid fifteen years. I couldn't have survived in the far-away Birch Bay house either. I am right where I need to be—in this capacious house with room for grandchildren to visit whenever, with room for my next chapter to take shape, whatever that will be.

I'm getting stiff and cold in this rocker. I get up, slowly, set the container of ashes on the shelf, crawl back into bed. I choose to be grateful, this time for the heated mattress pad that my friend Carrie bought for me after Bob died. I'd mentioned how cold the bed was now without him, how my feet felt like blocks of ice without him next to me—and voila!—she had solved that problem.

The digital clock ticks on. It's past 3:00 a.m. now. The owl outside is quiet. I am longing for sleep, and it's not happening. Exasperated, I picture sleep as an energetic little imp, teasing me, dancing away from me, always just out of reach, refusing to grant even a few hours of blessed unconsciousness.

I roll over in bed, punch the pillow, and finally flop on my back and stare wide-eyed at the ceiling. Thoughts tumble unbidden through my mind like laundry in a tumble dryer. It has been a difficult week, filled with meetings with accountants, with Troia Foods' owners, with our personal financial planner, every one of them lovely and helpful, but all speaking in terminology I barely grasped. Taken together, it's been a firehose of information, critically important information about our business as well as my finances that I should understand. I act as if I understand, but the truth is I can barely pull myself together to even attend these meetings. I roll over again, seeking comfort where there is none. Oh, where is Bob? He knows all this stuff! He knew what the plan was. He knew how to execute the plan.

I toss and turn from one side to the other. My mental tumble dryer picks up speed. What's happening with our headquarters building downtown? Did we get any graffiti today? Could Bob's killer be part of a gang? Would a gang target our building? My mind races, my pulse quickens, my heartbeat zooms. Could gang members look up assessor's records and learn where I live? Yes, Bob's killer is in jail now on $100,000 bond, but what if he—or others acting for him—posts bond and is out and about for the twelve or eighteen months it may take before the case goes to trial? We don't know what criminal connections he might have. What if, what if? Do. Not. Think. But thoughts keep tumbling, finally churning up one that torments me: what Bob's body looked like after dying from the blunt force trauma of a forty-miles-per-hour impact, what he looked like after being slammed into by a killer on a motorcycle-turned-missile.

I mentally slam the door on that thought and flop over again. Did I cry today? Did I laugh? Is the 401K up or down? Do I have any chin hairs that need plucking? Exasperation mounts: What other all-important thoughts will intrude tonight? I think of the fast-approaching morrow, its meetings, its tasks. It takes a lot of effort to walk onward with a shattered heart. Yet walk onward I will.

The sheets feel rough tonight, unwelcoming. I adopt yet another sleep position—on my back, right arm outstretched, palm facing the ceiling. I hope an angel will touch my hand in the night and reassure me I am not alone. I don't need to see an angel to believe they are about, and I do believe they can help us.

And then I see Bob. I am dreaming—am I dreaming? He is right there. He is so real. He's behind a sheen of falling water. He's in perfect physical shape, all his teeth in place, no sign of impact, not a bruise to be seen. His hair is brown and thick, no gray at the temples. He's about thirty years old.

I gasp. The rippling waterfall between us is glimmering, beautiful.

He communicates without speaking. *I am completely okay. I am doing fine.* No need for words in his world. I get his emphatic message.

And then message number two, delivered casually from my happy, healthy, young husband behind the shifting curtain of water. *It was probably a bit of a shock to some people that I left so abruptly.*

What?! Then understanding floods through me. He didn't have to know how painful his departure was to his family, his business associates, his friends. He did not see the tears. He did not see the people who literally fell to the floor when they heard. He does not see me walking around like a zombie, catatonic, trying to act normal for the kids, the grandkids, all the family. He is fine, and he's just musing, *hmm . . . must have been a shock, that abrupt departure.* I feel the sincere intent of this second message. He is comforting me, and for the first time in four months, I do not feel panicked, lost, alone, overwhelmed.

But there's more. Bob, his handsome, unlined face wreathed in kindness, delivers a third and final message. *Marth, everything is going to be fine.*

Oh! I don't have to worry about the upended retirement plans, the business we owned for decades and now have sold, our devastated sons and daughters-in-law and grandchildren, the finances, the houses, an empty and barren future without him. None of that. Everything is going to be fine. He didn't elaborate. He didn't need to. I understand fully. Everything is going to be fine. Bob has told me it is. And he knows. He has seen the other side.

The falling water dimmed and Bob's physical being was no more.

I awoke at seven, still feeling wrapped in his presence. He'd delivered his "all is well" message three times, just as important messages are communicated in the Gospels.

He was right. I'd been acting like Martha in the Gospel of Luke, worried and upset by many things, flitting around trying to solve problems, freaking out needlessly. Better to be like the smart sister Mary: Just sit at the feet of Jesus and know everything is going to be fine.

I roll out of bed, shower, dress, go downstairs. I start coffee, its familiar aroma filling the slowly warming kitchen. I glance out of the window toward the lake. Clouds, shifting sun, forty degrees. I tap my phone to see my calendar for the day: an early appointment with the accountant, a couple hours' worth of tasks at the business downtown, get to the store for groceries because the kids are coming tomorrow.

I wrap my hands around my warm cup and sip coffee. I pause, filling my memory with Bob's presence last night. Yes, walk onward I will, because everything is going to be fine.

January 27, 2023

## The Valentine's Day Store

Logan, age seven, clears his lunch plate from the table, slots it into my dishwasher's lower rack, and races to pick up his iPad.

"Yes, Logan, you may have screen time for an hour," I call after him, but he's vanished around the corner to the den. Zoey, age five, slides her little behind toward the front of her chair, stretches her legs toward the kitchen floor, lands on her feet, then picks up her plate and follows suit.

"Nana, I want to draw," Zoey says.

I nod, wipe off my kitchen table, and quickly dry it as Zoey fetches paper and markers. It's Thursday, which in Bellingham means early-release day for schoolchildren, so Logan and Zoey spend Thursday afternoons at my house. As always, I work at being brave and upbeat around them, but they know. Kids are far more attuned than we think.

I'm grateful these two are routinely in my life and in my house, but even so, most days this house is far too big and far too empty. Bob and I bought this lovely place just two months before he was killed with an eye toward frequent visits from family and friends. Now, most of the time, I'm rattling around its several thousand square feet and eating dinner alone.

I've been hatching a plan to address that. Now, as I hear the "ping, ping" from Logan's screen in the den and watch Zoey draw, my mind goes back to my big-house situation. One solution in particular appeals to me, what I call the "Golden Girls' house." Remember the sitcom, *The Golden Girls*, a show about four older women who shared a home in Miami? It aired on NBC from 1985 to 1992. Actresses Bea Arthur, Rue McClanahan, Estelle Getty, and the incomparable Betty White were in it. What if I took the big "bonus room" area above the garage and remodeled it into a separate living space? What if I also occasionally rented one of the main house's remaining four bedrooms to a college girl? My extra space here could become a blessing for someone else. I wouldn't be eating dinner alone every night, and there'd be someone else bumbling around here if I wanted to chat or she wanted to chat, or we could just coexist in companiable silence. Plus, with me spending a lot of time at my Arizona home, it's not smart to leave my Bellingham house empty. I could make it a Golden Girls' house. I love this idea!

"Nana, Nana," Zoey says, tugging my sleeve, pushing a wisp of light brown hair from her face. I realize she's been trying to get my attention for some time.

I snap out of my Golden Girls' reverie and back to the present. "Yes, sweetheart?" I say, looking at her picture. She's drawn a storefront, I can see that, and two stick figures holding hands. One figure is pink, one is blue. "It's lovely, Zoey," I say, pulling my chair closer to hers, putting my arm around her shoulders. "Tell me about it."

"Well, Nana," Zoey says in a businesslike tone, "this is the Valentine's Day Store in Heaven. When you die, PapaBob is going to come and find you and hold your hand and take you to the

Valentine's Day Store in Heaven, because he loves you and he will be so happy to see you again."

I am once again struck by the emotional intelligence of children. I think of the Bible quote that reminds us of this, Isaiah 11:6, "And a little child shall lead them." And here is Zoey leading me, taking me from grief to solace, from an earthly outlook to an eternal one, saying what I need to hear.

I look around my kitchen, already decorated with Zoey's many previous drawings on the theme of "how things are now," with PapaBob and the family dog, with angels and sunshine and smiles all around.

This drawing on the table now of The Valentine's Day Store in Heaven will be laminated and kept forever.

January through May 2023

# Staying on the Sparkle Spectrum

"Here's to the Golden Girls!" I raise my glass of pinot grigio, grinning at my new-ish friend Courtney Jenkins across the restaurant table. It's a wet, cold day in January 2023, and we're at Anthony's at Squalicum Harbor in Bellingham, comfortably full of Pacific Northwest seafood. Wintry rain patters against our booth's window. I'm pleased to be out of my lonely house, eating dinner with a friend in this restaurant with the low, friendly sound of other patrons' conversation humming around us. Courtney and I sip well-chilled wine from glasses that show a sheen of condensation; I enjoy white wine and spare my liver for celebratory moments like this.

"Here's to your Golden Girls' house!" Courtney says, her glass meeting mine with a clink.

I take a sip. The wine's crisp flavors of apple and pear float over my tongue. "Although you're a little young to be a Golden Girl," I say with a wry smile.

I had met Courtney three months ago when I volunteered to help paint interior walls at the Armory, a castle-like building that served as a military drill hall during both world wars, and later as a roller-skating rink. It had been virtually empty for decades before Courtney and her business partner Craig Cooper teamed up to start their new business in it, Armory Pickleball.

Back in November, Courtney and I, both wielding paintbrushes inside the vast, echo-y building, immediately hit it off. She had never met Bob and was horrified by his sudden death. She quickly became a friend, the kind who would "stand in the gap" with me, who'd call, check in, ask "Want to go for coffee?" About ten years younger than I, Courtney's kind heart and listening ear became a lifeline. I never felt the need to don a "mask," to act as if I was doing fine when I wasn't. She was genuine and so true to herself that I instinctively felt I could share my true self with her.

Tonight at Anthony's we're talking about what could work as a living arrangement. She is seeking a new situation; I am looking for a solution to my capacious house. Soon enough, it is settled: In April, Courtney will move into the blue bedroom next to my master suite; her two teen sons will each take one of the remaining upstairs bedrooms with the three of them sharing the hall bathroom.

This situation with my first (albeit young) Golden Girl, would work out even better than we had thought. Her sons were delightful and energetic, with an upbeat vibe that permeated the house. Courtney's rent helped me stay afloat during the tumultuous months of the buyout of Dairy Distributing and during my newly launched, extensive remodel of the sizable "bonus room" over my garage. Yes, I was going forward full steam to make that space into a fully appointed guest suite with a fabulous walk-out deck overlooking the lake. I was making room for future Golden Girls!

Courtney, always caring, always plainspoken, looked out for me. If she saw I wasn't eating, she'd make a big protein-packed breakfast and convince me to eat it. We had a little inside joke: Every other day or so, she'd check in with me, asking, "How are we on the sparkle spectrum? Are we feeling upbeat? Or is this a rough moment?" She favored the phrase, "You can't make this shit up!" a saying I'd soon find out would get a lot of use from both of us.

When the over-the-garage space was finished, Courtney moved in there but still cooked and spent time with me and the boys in the main house.

Courtney and her boys lived with me for thirteen months. During that time, we spent a lot of time together and a lot of time apart, as I was at my Arizona home for much of the year. When we were all in the Bellingham house, though I was still buffeted by waves of traumatic grief, I did my darndest to hold it together in the house's shared spaces.

Only twice during those months did I burst into Courtney's space with news that was too much for me to handle alone.

The first time was in May 2023, eight months into this grief stuff. I'd still sometimes awaken in amazement that this was my life. Before Bob's death, I was so normal, so happy, an all-American wife and mother and grandma living the dream, getting ready for retirement. Then, in a moment, in the screech of a crash miles away on a road in Skagit County, I ceased to be that woman. I became this woman, alone in her rocking chair in the dark with the metal container of her husband's ashes on her lap and a pile of books about grief on her nightstand.

Now, eight months in, with the initial shock and fog worn off but the pain intensifying and suicidal thoughts creeping in, I knew I needed professional help. I found it in a lovely Christian counselor named Karen. With Karen, over two, two-hour sessions, I learned I was "stuffing" my grief, that my natural desire to not feel pain would eventually boil up. Though I was understandably fearful of its power, refusing to allow myself to feel pain would not serve me. Karen helped me recognize that I was a pretty good actress, that I donned a "mask" to protect myself in public, which was exhausting.

So far, so good! I looked forward to my third session with Karen.

The evening before my appointment, my cell phone buzzed. I recognized Karen's name, picked up my phone.

"Martha? Martha?" Karen's voice was frantic. Worse, her breath was coming in short gasps.

*Oh no, oh no.* I knew this shallow breathing, this inability to catch your breath. I knew it from living with traumatic grief.

"I can't meet tomorrow!" Karen managed that much.

"What?! What's happened?" Now I was as frantic as she. As much as I needed her, I tried to make it better. "Karen, no problem, we can reschedule."

"No, no, I'm closing my practice, I'm moving . . ." Karen stopped, fought for breath. "My daughter! She was hiking in Utah, she fell off a cliff, she broke her neck, she's dead."

It was my turn to gasp, to grip the kitchen countertop, to drop into a chair. Now I was having trouble breathing. Through the phone, I heard a tangle of chaotic voices, then steady voices. I recognized those voices, that sound, as support officers. They were right there with Karen, in these first moments of shock, horror, chaos, disbelief.

"I have to go," Karen choked out, and hung up.

That's it, that's all I could take. In that moment, I needed another human. A friend. Courtney. I barged into her room, barely able to breathe, crying out this news. And Courtney hugged me. A big hug. Courtney said, "You can't make this shit up!"

She's right. You can't.

September 25, 2022, through June 2023

# Knocked off the Sparkle Spectrum

Not knowing was agonizing. During the weeks after Bob's death, when his killer was still on the loose with a charge of vehicular homicide against him, I didn't know where he was or what he might do. Was he affiliated with the gang graffiti that showed up on our building downtown? (Not just once; our place was "tagged" on three different nights.) Would he find out where I lived? Would he follow me? Was he even now watching me? No way to know.

These thoughts leapt unbidden into my mind, no matter how I tried to squash them. We didn't know anything about this man other than his driving record and what we'd seen of him on the police cam during a previous apprehension for reckless driving. We didn't know if he was suicidal, if he knew we were praying for him, if he knew we were forgiving him.

Then, in November 2022, forty-five excruciating days after the Horrendous Event, he made a wrong move, and the State Patrol apprehended him without incident at a convenience store in the town of Snohomish. He was booked into Skagit County Community Justice Center on a $100,000 bond.

Now the not-knowing took on a new form: delays. A court date was set, delayed, reset, delayed. Every time I heard from the court staff it knocked me completely off the sparkle spectrum. But now it's set again and will surely go forward, so I book a flight from Arizona to Bellingham. Oops, never mind, delayed again.

This went on for seven exasperating months. At one point in January 2023, we had a big meeting at my Bellingham home with the entire prosecution team and sixteen family members and close friends. The meeting, though necessary, ramped up the stress on me. Before the meeting and afterward—but not during, thankfully—I melted into masses of tears. Afterward, for the first time but not the last, my body rebelled against the chronic stress by producing a sudden, gushing, bloody nose.

During this meeting there was talk of a plea bargain to avoid a full-on jury trial, which would have been beyond awful to endure.

Days, weeks ticked by. On again, off again, nothing settled yet . . . and then the phone call came from the court. There would be no trial; the defendant had signed the plea bargain. We family members were requested to attend the sentencing and present a victim impact statement. After which, Bob's killer would be handcuffed and taken to prison for thirteen years.

I'm at home in Bellingham the day the court calls with the date for the sentencing. My friend and housemate Courtney is in her room working on her laptop, managing her thriving start-up pickleball business. Her teen sons are at school. That day, my hand sweats as I hold my phone, as I hear the court staffer give me the news; she is as kind as ever. I tell myself, breathe deep; my body wants to hyperventilate but I don't let it.

The court staffer continues. "The hearing, the sentencing, is ten days from now," she says, "at 10:00 a.m. on Friday, June 23, in the Skagit County courthouse in Mount Vernon."

That date is my thirty-ninth wedding anniversary. Yes, I will meet Bob's killer on my first wedding anniversary without Bob.

For only the second time in the thirteen months that we lived in the same house, I go to Courtney's room, knock, hear her affirmative reply. Within a split second I'm in there, this news bubbling up and out of me like a surging hot-springs in a Pacific Northwest forest. Once again, in this moment, I need a friend. Once again, I need to hear what I know she will say.

"You can't make this shit up!" Courtney says, enveloping me in a hug.

*Note to reader: I meant to change this quote, writing it, "You can't make this stuff up!" My dear departed mother-in-law, among others, would be appalled if I wrote "shit." But I changed my mind. Sometimes, you just have to say shit.*

May through June 2023

# The Sentencing

The message from our family would be one of grace and forgiveness. I was adamant about this. In the weeks before the June twenty-third sentencing of Bob's killer, which we would all attend, I repeated this message often.

We were familiar with the Gospel of Matthew 18:21-22, in which Peter asks Jesus how many times he should forgive his brother who has sinned against him—seven times? Jesus answers, "seventy times seven," and Christians understand this to mean we are called to forgive limitlessly, infinitely, without end.

Of course, understanding that intellectually and feeling it emotionally when your heart is broken are two different matters. But we would do it. It was the right thing to do, the only thing to do. From childhood, each of us had recited from The Lord's Prayer: "Forgive us our trespasses as we forgive those who trespass against us." Forgiveness would deliver us from the evil of anger and hate. It would be essential for our healing.

Essential, too, were the therapists and psychologists who helped our family. First, on Day Two After Bob's Death, our therapist Randy told us we would all experience grief in different ways. That would become more important as time went on.

Next was my counselor Karen, whom I found in May 2023 when I was buried under tidal waves—make that tsunami waves—of grief, trying to choose to be happy and so exhausted, so *done* with it all. Before Karen, I was waking up every morning and feeling disappointed that I hadn't died in my sleep. I found a lifeline in Karen, who helped me identify my root fear: abandonment by everyone in the world if I couldn't pull myself together and be happy again. Karen taught me to "feel the feels," lest I become murderously angry. (Thank you, Karen. I hope your grief journey over your daughter's death has been smoother since at least, you have experience in managing grief. Not that it's easier. But awareness is a good thing.)

Also, our family members were so kindly treated by their employers. Bob's death was all over the Seattle news and even picked up by a national broadcast. The "no chase" rule for law enforcement had been a hot topic for a while. (In 2021, Washington state increased the threshold for evidence required for police pursuits, while limiting the types of crimes that could result in chases. Unsurprisingly, crime rose. The law was amended in 2023 and amended further in 2024.) And here we had a Bellingham husband, father, and grandfather, a business owner and CEO, massacred while safe-riding in an eight-thousand-rider motorcycle rally while in the quaint little town of Anacortes.

At our family's various workplaces, this was understood to be much more than just a "sorry your parent died" situation. Many days of bereavement leave were granted.

"What do you *mean* you're not coming?" Our son Tory was dumbstruck that his older brother Tyler would not attend the sentencing. "How can you not be there? We've got to be there!"

"It's a weekday," Tyler responded, his voice distant, his face closed. "I have to work."

"Are you sure Troia Foods won't let you off for a morning?" Tory was horrified, then as light dawned, furious. His eyes narrowed. "No way would they keep you from this!"

Once again, experts helped. A counselor explained that traumatic grief triggers a fight or flight response.

Tory chose to fight. I had encouraged anyone in the family to speak or write whatever they felt needed to be said, and Tory wrote the victim impact statement, which became our family's message.

Tyler chose flight. He'd forgiven the killer in front of the whole family months ago. He'd made his peace. Now he was done with the nightmare.

As the counselor emphasized to us, everyone chooses his own grief path.

Soon enough, with grace and acceptance flowing both ways, we came to understand Tyler and Stephanie's choice. Through the day of sentencing and long after, therapists continued to help us, together and individually. With all their tools and methods, over time, they would help us feel hopeful of someday having a good life again.

On Friday morning, June 23, the rest of us settled into our seats in a dark-paneled room in the courthouse complex in the Skagit County town of Mount Vernon. Others were with us: my sisters, high school friends, recent friends, the motorcycle pals who'd ridden with Bob on numerous multi-state adventures. A sister-in-law spoke, saying she thought that with the gravity and timing of his previous offenses, defendant Michael E. Icenhour should have been incarcerated at the time of the September twenty-fifth collision. Whatcom Business Alliance played the five-minute video made for Bob's Lifetime Achievement Award at their gala in March. Then, through shoulder-quaking sobs, Tory stood and delivered his impact statement:

"I am not here today to get even with you. An eye for an eye is never productive, though a part of me wishes you had also died that day (I'm sure a part of you wishes that as well). My father taught me at a young age that actions have consequences, and I've had my share of painful consequences, but I've learned and grown from them. In this instance, your reckless actions led to reckless consequences—I am speaking to you today, hoping you learn from your mistakes so you do not hurt anyone else in the way you've hurt me and my family.

"Your blatant disregard for those around you is frightful. You have shown time and time again that your "live fast/die young" mentality is the life you have chosen. Let me be clear—you can choose a different lifestyle, and you have thirteen years to figure it out. There usually comes a point in every man's life when he looks in the mirror and says, 'I can do better.' Your actions the day you killed my dad were childish and foolish. I know you didn't set out to kill my dad, but it really sucks that it was him caught in your moment of complete senselessness. You have a lot of time to think about the harm your actions have caused. I beg you—do better.

"My dad was a truly good person. I'm not just saying that because he was my dad, but because you could see it by the people he surrounded himself with. He was a faithful husband, an incredible father and family man, and he had friends everywhere he went. We miss him every day.

"I have two kids of my own—now three-and-a-half, and one-and-a-half. My dad missed his last grandchild's first birthday because you killed him. Thankfully Dad had a chance to hold both of my kids, but I am heartbroken that they will be too young to remember their PapaBob or to experience the joy of his laugh and the love he gave so freely. We were already looking forward to getting older and being able to attend PapaBob's sponsored 'Grandpa Camp.' My dad loved being a grandparent so much that he planned weeks full of activities. Because of your actions that day, my kids will never get that experience.

"To be frank, thirteen years does not feel like justice to me. The crimes you have committed are despicable and I'm sure you are embarrassed by that list. You know it, we all know it. You should be locked up for life—you have three strikable offenses. I don't know how nor why you survived that accident, but I am hopeful that you do what you need to do to turn your life around. Get the help you need and *do better*."

Tory, steady now, took his seat. The room stayed silent, save for a few muffled sobs; almost everyone in the room was struggling to hold it together. After a few moments, the judge spoke, addressing the defendant directly.

"This family has given you a true gift," the judge said. "Let me say, in this setting this is something we rarely see. This family is offering you the gift of forgiveness. I hope you use the time ahead of you to understand what that means."

Case closed. Court dismissed. It was over.

Part One of our nightmare was behind us. Before us lay Part Two, the next mountain to climb: rediscovering laughter, rekindling joy, rebuilding lives.

September 25, 2023

# I Can Scale Cliffs, I Can Leap Chasms

My coffee sits untouched on the kitchen table before me. I no longer realize it's there. I am meeting someone new, a widow who has rebuilt her life, and my coffee is cooling as I listen, rapt, to her story.

Debbie is slim, blond, and vivacious, just a couple of years younger than I. Her beloved husband Owen died six years ago after a two-year battle with brain cancer. I am visiting Debbie at her home in Quincy, Illinois, of all places. How did this come about? Debbie is the sister-in-law of my dear Bellingham friend Carrie; Carrie and her husband John wanted me to meet Debbie, so Carrie, John, and I are now spending a few days in the Midwest. At this moment, Carrie and John are out for a walk in the gorgeous morning sunshine as Debbie and I talk about life after the untimely deaths of our husbands.

Debbie pours a touch of cream into her coffee, stirs it. "Owen was a fabulous husband and an incredible father to our two kids," Debbie says. "He had the most generous heart."

She sips her brew, savors it, smiles at me. "My daughter and I built our business on that foundation of generosity. We are so grateful for our customers, our whole community. We partner with various foundations and put a lot of effort into supporting local events."

Debbie tells me more about Owen, a man of faith who liked to organize family and friends to go camping or boating, who had fun raising money for good causes. I smile at that. He sounds a lot like Bob. As I keep listening, I see that Debbie is not only a widow but a powerful woman as well as the very definition of a servant leader: someone who puts others first and helps them grow, who uses her power to serve her community.

I soon realize two things: one, right now Debbie is helping me more than she knows, and two, no way should I have let this coffee grow cold. Debbie supplied our coffee this morning from the business she and her daughter started in 2020, Carter's Coffee Bar, and indeed the coffee is outstanding. I learn that Carter's Coffee Bar now has multiple locations and employees.

But first, the backstory: Debbie and Owen lived most of their adult lives in Lake Stevens, Washington, where they raised their family. As their children moved out and launched their own lives, she and Owen stayed in Lake Stevens, anticipating retirement and travel. After his untimely death, Debbie moved across the country to Illinois to be near her daughter, and together they launched a business.

I wrap my hands around my coffee mug and glance out the window at undulating fields of corn, the stalks showing mostly long, green leaves but with their yellowing edges heralding cooler autumn nights. Downstate Illinois, with its miles of sunny cornfields stretching to a flat horizon, is vastly different from the endless gray-green of the coniferous, mountainous Pacific Northwest. Sitting here in

Debbie's beautiful farmhouse kitchen looking out at a sea of corn, I see that her move here required a deep well of courage along with a leap of faith.

I can tap into that courage, that faith within myself. I think of something I read recently on Facebook in a private community called "We Are Widow Warriors" (author not noted): "You don't heal with time, you heal with intention." Yes, we are warriors. I will soldier on, intentionally choosing to heal.

I bring my focus back to Debbie, who is saying things I want to hear, things I need to hear, especially today, September 25, 2023, the first anniversary of Bob's death. I knew I couldn't spend the first anniversary of the Horrendous Event at home. I knew I needed to be thoroughly distracted, completely engaged with others on this day of all days. I'm grateful to Carrie and John, who conceived this trip, who urged me to come with them to visit Debbie. (After a few days here, all of us will go to the vacation destination of Branson, Missouri.)

I'm so glad we came. Everything Debbie says, everything she *is*, gives me hope. And there's more good news! I just got word from family back home that a new baby for our extended family was born earlier this morning, at exactly 12:05 a.m. today, September 25.

The birth of this precious girl forever redeems this date for the entire extended Bray clan. Now, going forward, our whole family will be able to celebrate this new life, this beautiful child, every September 25 instead of remembering it only as the day Bob was taken from us. The baby's birth is even more fabulous, because this couple, our nephew and his wife, had previously been told by doctors they would likely be unable to have children. Yet here she is, the miracle child.

Oh, and one more thing: Despite labor starting on September 23 (and lasting thirty grueling hours), the baby waited an extra five minutes so she could land on September 25.

As my Bellingham friend and housemate Courtney would say, you can't make this stuff up.

*(Note to reader: This time I'm using the word "stuff" in honor of my dear deceased mother-in-law, whose name today was bestowed as a middle name on the new baby.)*

Tonight, as the first anniversary of Bob's death comes to a close, I head toward bed. I will sleep on an air mattress in a spacious extra room on the first floor of Debbie's house. John and Carrie are settling onto another roomy air mattress. We chat a little, and once again I'm glad of their company, glad I'm not alone tonight. After our talk stills, I make a conscious effort to think about the good things that happened today. I think about the hope Debbie poured into me along with her excellent coffee.

I have a little reading light by my mattress, small enough not to bother Carrie and John, so I pick up my book of daily devotions, *Jesus Calling* by Sarah Young. Settling down on my pillow, I open it to today's reading. "Pour all of your energy into trusting Me," it begins. It goes on to say baby steps of trust are simple, but giant steps are another matter altogether that require leaping chasms, scaling cliffs, trudging through the valley of the shadow of death.

I put the book down, stunned. It's as if this author knew what my year has been like, as if she knew this date would be hard, as if she knew I have spent twelve months in the valley of the shadow of death.

I turn off the light, roll over, take deep, steady breaths. Today is over. Today's date, September 25, was a hike through a dark valley, but I got through it. There will be more valleys. I will walk on, trusting, knowing He is with me. As Young puts it, there will be chasms, but I can leap across them. There will be cliffs, but I can scale them.

I can do this. I am not traveling alone.

Sept. 26, 2023—So, off we go on Year Two, rocking Option B, heading off to Branson, choosing to be happy. I start this second year fortified by Debbie's example and celebrating as new people come into my life at the right time, with the right purpose. During the drive south through Illinois and into Missouri, I think about my Bellingham home, about the huge remodel of the bonus room space over the three-car garage. It's almost done now. I am building a great Golden Girls' house with attractive, rentable space so I won't have to live by myself.

I am not alone, in more ways than one.

April 2024

# Take Me Out to the Ballgame

Spring in Bellingham for our family means baseball. Bob played as a high schooler at Sehome High School and, later, on community leagues. I love remembering his out-of-the-park home run when he was forty-six at Joe Martin Stadium in Bellingham. A great moment!

We're a baseball family, for sure. Younger son Tory played throughout Bellingham High School and beyond, in between running his lawn-mowing business. Older son Tyler lettered in varsity baseball in high school and hit numerous home runs, one off Jake Locker's pitching. (Jake's a Whatcom County boy who was drafted by the Los Angeles Angels but played college football for the University of Washington and later quarterbacked for the NFL's Tennessee Titans.)

Today, Tyler's down in front of us on the sidelines of the ballfield at Lummi Nation Community Park north of Bellingham, helping coach Logan's youth baseball team. The nine-year-old boys on the field are adorable, looking like miniature New York Yankees in their white uniforms with black stripes and black knee socks. Goodness, can they get any cuter?! I'm in the bleachers sitting with a gaggle of friends and family, including Zoey, who's running up and down the bleacher steps with a herd of half-a-dozen little girls, all younger sibs of the boys on the field.

I shift on the hard seat and glance skyward. Fourth inning, and the rain's holding off. Good. The little girls, a couple of them inexplicably wearing Disney princess costumes, sprint down the bleachers and onto the field perimeter where they kick a soccer ball around before running toward the moms in the concession stand. I smile. They're like colorful butterflies, flitting around the park perimeter—though butterflies have longer attention spans. The little girls do everything but watch the game, gabbing, hopping, laughing, playing wherever they happen to alight.

Like the little girls, my mind wanders from the game on the field. I think of a movie I saw months ago, the docudrama, *After Death* by Angel Studios, in which scientists, authors, and survivors of near-death experiences discuss the afterlife, the big question of what happens after we die. I remember one man, revived ninety minutes after his "death," which was coded as such by medical professionals. The man reported that Heaven was better than Earth, emphasizing, "If I could have stayed in Heaven, I would have chosen that." This, despite returning to a great earthly life with a loyal, loving wife, children, and grandchildren.

I shift on the bleacher seat again, my grandmother-radar scanning for the girls. I see them playing over by the press-box. They're fine. I look toward the field. Nothing much happening with the game right now either. My mind drifts back to the movie. Before I saw it, I would weep at what Bob was missing: every grandchild's birthday, every fiery sunset over Bellingham Bay, every silvery full moon over Lake Whatcom, every boating adventure with lifelong friends, every holiday with treasured family. Thinking of all that, sadness would start in my heart and seep into every cell of my being. But now, after seeing this movie, I'm not sad but happy for him. Even if he could come back, he'd prefer to stay in Heaven. It's hard for me to swallow, but true, I think.

Back to the game. Gray clouds scud across the sky. Still no rain. I focus on the boys. The opposing team is on the field. Our team is at bat. Tyler crouches next to a boy who's about to come up to bat. Tyler's a master at instilling the fundamentals of throwing, catching, and hitting, and that training shows now, even in boys as young as this. The first boy hits a double to applause from the bleachers. The next boy singles to bigger applause.

Players are now on third and first bases. Tyler is standing well back now as Logan comes to bat. My heart swells at the sight of Logan, our little one who's not so little anymore, at the concentration on his young face, at the numeral 5 on the back of his uniform under the proud lettering spelling "Bray."

The first pitch is outside the "box" and Logan doesn't swing. The second is as well. Logan, brows knitting together, his eye on the ball, doesn't swing. The third pitch and *crack!*—Logan's bat connects hard, sending a line drive through center field. Logan takes off running with every ounce of speed he has, rounding first, second, third. Home run! The stands erupt in applause, everyone jumping to their feet, laughing, clapping. Stephanie, my daughter-in-law and Logan's mom, high-fives her mom and dad, Logan's other grandparents. Logan's first home run! His first home run! You only get one first, and this is it, this golden, singular moment of childhood.

Oh! Bob would've loved this! I cannot stop my tears. Where is Bob? Why can't he be here with us? I no longer see the green field, the boys, the white uniforms, the gray sky. Through tears, I flee the bleachers, the park. I can't cry in public like this. I can't believe Bob's not here. Why did it have to happen?

Outside the gate, I lean against the chain-link fence. I make a valiant effort to stem my tears and corral my swirling thoughts. I take one deep breath, then another. I remember, even if Bob could come back, he'd choose to stay where he is. Is Heaven better than watching your first grandchild hit his first home run? Yes. I hold that thought.

Logan's first home run at Lummi fields happened early in the season. Our little all-star went on to hit his second homer at an away game in the Shoreline suburb of Seattle. That day, after Logan's homer, his uncle Tory went over to the dugout to hug Logan, to congratulate him, to say the words that PapaBob would say. That day I wasn't the only one tearing up in the car with the rest of the family driving back to Tory's house. But that day, I thought, *Logan is going to go right on hitting home runs, and by the third one, I'll probably be okay.*

Logan's third home run was back at Lummi fields in Whatcom County. The same crew was there, the same gaggle of family and friends. All the team parents know how challenging these months have been for us. They've always been so kind. Among the hometown faces at Lummi fields that day, I saw some of Bob's baseball friends from his high school days; some of them teared up when they saw me.

But I did not. Logan had just hit his third home run. I was applauding. I was happy for all of us, including Bob, who is in Heaven experiencing something even better than this golden, transcendent moment here on this ballfield on Earth.

It was Logan's third home run, and I was okay.

Spring 2024

# From Horror Movie to Rom-Com

Bellingham, with its population of ninety-seven thousand, is somehow still a small town. Consider this interaction in the staff lunchroom at Barron Heating, an HVAC contractor in our county. (Over the years, Bob and I had hired them to redo four fireplaces in our various houses. I'm pretty sure we put a few of their kids through college with our expenditures.)

Back to the staff room. A friend who was to play pickleball with me later, also a Barron employee, mentions in this lunchroom that she is going to meet Martha Bray tonight at Armory Pickleball. Nods all around as other employees munch sandwiches and swig kombucha. (Apparently, everyone at Barron knows who I am. That may have something to do with our fireplaces.)

One employee swallows a bite of apple before asking, "Is Martha dating anyone yet?"

"I don't think so," my pickleball friend says.

The other employee's response: "What's wrong with her?"

When this conversation is relayed to me—kindly—I am taken aback. Not only that Bob and I most definitely spent too much on fireplaces, but seriously, what *is* wrong with me?

This becomes my wake-up call. Do I want to spend the rest of my life alone? No. Is a man going to show up in my driveway riding a white horse to rescue me? No (but maybe . . .?) It is now nineteen months since the Horrendous Event, and I need to take action.

But the idea of dating strangers after thirty-eight years of a secure and happy married life is beyond daunting. I have no idea how to go about it, how it works, how people interact romantically online. I now have a total of exactly two single adult male acquaintances in my entire universe of friends where virtually everyone is married.

I sit in front of my laptop and type "eHarmony" in the browser. I have no idea what I'm doing. I do it anyway.

So it begins, my life from horror movie to rom-com. Let me introduce you to the men who were to be my potential dates, and maybe someday, my potential mate. They are numbered. And just so you know, most of them are named Dave. Really.

I fill out the profile on eHarmony. It's helpful. You put in your interests, your religion, how many kids you have and whether any live at home. You list your parameters: non-smoker, light drinker, age. Men on the site input their interests and parameters as well. The men who will be introduced as matches will have many commonalities with me.

At this stage, the only identifying information either of us gets is the other's first name.

This causes an immediate bookkeeping conundrum for me. How will I keep them straight in my phone contacts since several men are replying? Plus, I need to keep them separate from any Daves I know from nonromantic areas of my life. I cannot mix up online dates with any real-life contacts.

I pause, drumming my fingers on my desk, thinking for a moment, then I hit on an idea. I will assign them all the same last name but number them in order of appearance. For the last name, I decide on "Ax Murderer." (Hey, a girl's gotta do what a girl's gotta do.)

With that personal organization system in place, I begin messaging on the eHarmony platform. I now know how this works. If the eHarmony messaging is comfortable, we move to texting on our own phone numbers. If that's working, we instigate an actual phone call. If that's still okay, we arrange a coffee shop venue and meet for real.

This led to what was to be my first live meet-up with Dave Ax Murderer #1, who said he worked at a global tech firm with a location in Seattle. We texted and chatted over a period of ten days before arranging to meet on a Friday afternoon at the coffee shop at Snoqualmie Falls, a scenic attraction with observation decks overlooking a 270-foot waterfall. It was convenient for him and for me, since I was already planning to spend the rest of the coming weekend with my younger son Tory's family at their home in the Seattle suburbs.

This could go well! I was looking forward to this Friday afternoon. The falls are always beautiful in the spring when they're roaring, bursting with spring snowmelt from the mountains, and on the phone, Dave Ax Murderer #1 was nice, funny, endearing, even.

The Wednesday before, I played pickleball with my friend Carolyn, who happens to work for the same huge tech firm. She thought it would be fun to look up Dave Ax Murderer #1 on the company website. (By that time, I had his last name.) The tech company has a couple thousand people in Seattle and tens of thousands in the country, but this particular Dave was not among them.

Thursday night on the phone with Dave Ax Murderer #1, while conversing about other things, I briefly asked him about his absence from the company site.

"What are you looking me up for?" Dave Ax Murderer #1's tone is pure anger. "What do you need to know about me that you can't ask me outright?"

I am caught completely off-guard. I shake my head briefly, not knowing what to say.

"What do you need to check me out for?" His voice escalates. "Why are you sneaking around behind my back?"

What? What? "I wasn't, it wasn't like that, really . . ." I say, but I am not allowed to speak because he is shouting over me.

"Well, you can forget about tomorrow afternoon because I want no part of anyone who thinks she needs to check on me!" He yells and ends the call.

Whoa. Whoa. I was about to say, I was just looking to understand more about your job. I thought you might be a subcontractor for that tech firm. But I never got the chance.

I stare at my silent phone. No meet-up after all. I feel deflated, even though I'm also pretty sure I dodged a bullet. What is with his anger?

That Friday, I skipped Snoqualmie Falls, drove to Tory and Katie's home, and spent the weekend with them and their two darling little ones. It was fine, and so was I. But whoa, dating as a widow is rough, and I haven't even started yet.

Spring 2024

# Best Wishes, You Seem Like a Nice Person

My next potential date, regrettably, is memorable for one thing: His name is not Dave. Greg Ax Murderer #2 and I texted several times, just long enough to realize we were not a match. His final goodbye is "Best wishes, you seem like a nice person."

I was to discover that saying is used so often with online dating, it's become cliché.

Never mind. Onward, ever onward. Next up is Dave Ax Murderer #3. He's told me he's a widower, he's five feet seven inches tall, he loves pickleball. Okay, I can work with this! Almost immediately, we arrange a pickleball meet-up to be followed by a light dinner at Panera Bread on Sunset Drive in Bellingham.

Oh my, what to wear? I stand in my bedroom in front of an open closet, frowning at my choices of sports skirts, realizing there's not a lot of difference among them. I grab a white skirt and blousy blue top to match my eyes, pull them on, and glance out the window to check the weather for the fourth time. I am dressing for my first date in forty years—thirty-eight years married, almost two years widowed—and my choice is pickleball skirts! On to other matters: Hair up or hair down? Visor or sunglasses for the game? I lean toward the mirror, checking my teeth for any scraps of spinach. Did I floss? Yes. All the important things. First impressions are important.

At Cornwall Park public courts, I see him, wave, walk over, smile, introduce myself. Instantly, I see he's not five foot seven. I am five feet six, and I'm taller than he is. Did I say first impressions are important? That's my first impression of him. Oh well. A court becomes available and we two quickly take one side.

As the afternoon progresses, we play together, we play on opposing courts, we play on neighboring courts. Dave Ax Murderer #3 seems nice enough, and he's a decent player. Of the thirty-five players rotating on and off the six courts, I know about half, and they quickly pick up on my first-date situation.

"Good for you, Martha!" murmurs one.

"Getting out there and meeting people, good job," whispers another, as we stoop to pick up a stray ball.

"You look great, go for it!" says another, smiling mischievously.

I'm grateful for all of them. They're cute about the date, and pickleball is always fun.

Dave Ax Murderer #3 and I drive separately to the restaurant. We meet at the restaurant door. I see he is actually about five feet four inches tall. Whatever. I smile as he opens the door for me.

"Dave, tell me more about yourself." I dab my mouth with a napkin. We've covered a few pleasantries already. Time to get to more important topics. Perhaps this widower and I have more in common than a height differential. Perhaps he'll tell me about his departed wife, how he's rebuilding his life after her untimely death. I smile encouragingly.

"My first wife died three months ago," Dave Ax Murderer #3 begins, putting down his half-eaten sandwich.

First wife? He hadn't mentioned the word "first" before. But he's continuing.

"She and I divorced twenty-five . . . no, twenty-seven years ago now," he says.

My eyes narrow. He presented himself online as a widower, but that's hardly the case. His fib about his height is paling next to this falsehood, this lie cloaked in a fact that actually hides the truth. I sip my Coke, my heart sinking.

I swallow hard. "Your first wife?" I inquire, keeping my voice light.

"Yeah, that didn't work out," Dave Ax Murderer #3 says, picking up that sandwich, chomping into it. I wait for him to finish before asking any more questions. Blessedly, he waits too, finishing his mouthful before carrying on. "My second wife, that was Susie, she was a screamer, I found that out pretty quick, we divorced after a couple of years."

"So, you've been single for more than twenty years?" I ask, but even as I say it, I'm pretty sure there's more, lots more, to come, and I am not wrong. Dave Ax Murderer #3 tells me about his past with wives number two, three, and four: bankruptcy, infidelities, screaming fights, some of which involved thrown plates. His last three wives are very much alive, and according to him, all of them are more or less crazy.

As he rattles on, telling stories about his exes, my heart sinks lower and lower until it seems as if it's laying on the floor under our booth. I think, *funny how it's always the divorced wife who's labeled crazy. Funny how the failed marriage is always her fault.* I prop my elbow on the table, rest my chin in my hand. I look at him, but my mind is elsewhere, thinking, *I am only sitting here because Bob is dead.* This is sad: the situation, the exes, the roaring dysfunction. This is really, really hard. I slump a little lower. Dave Ax Murderer #3 doesn't notice.

I wait for an opening, see it, and jump in, saying, "Well, I have to get going."

"Can we meet again?" Dave Ax Murderer #3 asks, hope lighting his eyes.

"No," I say, donning my warm-up sweater from the pickleball game, gathering my purse, standing up. "I see we're not a match. But I wish you the best, you seem like a nice person."

Laughter bubbles up now amid a tangle of comments, such as, "Could be useful down the line," and "Gems, huh? We like it!"

I laugh too, delighted to be among friends, happy in their fun-loving company. "Listen to these texts," I say, tapping and scrolling. "Here they are." I read aloud what he's sent over the preceding days. His words show emotional intelligence, relationship skills, and a genuine interest in me.

My gang on loungers is now swooning. Keep going, they say. I do.

"He asks where I like to travel, which places I like best, what I do for fun with my grandchildren." I scroll on. "He knows a lot about jewelry. Here's a photo of him at the Tate Modern art gallery in London." I pass my phone around again.

When it returns to me, I lay back on the lounger. I have decided. "He and I have texted enough," I proclaim. "Tonight, I'll arrange a meet-up with Ax Murderer #4 for when I get back to Washington."

That evening, during my texting banter back and forth with him about a future meeting, Ax Murderer #4 sends another photo of himself, this one with a Washington state ferry in the background amid the weather and muted gray light of the Pacific Northwest. He is dashing, with that smile, rounded glasses, curly hair, and just a hint of fashionable gray stubble. Goodness!

Around my breakfast table next day, I share the latest pic with my girl gang. I also send it to my sister-in-law and niece in Washington.

I was to find out later how that photo was received. My twenty-six-year-old niece looked at the photo, asked about his story. She went silent, set her mouth in a firm line, went to her laptop, and did an AI search of the image.

She discovered the photo of the dashing man with the ferry in the background had been lifted from a random LinkedIn profile of an innocent, actual Seattle doctor who was not on any dating website.

I sent the image back to Ax Murderer #4 with a question mark. He did not reply. Not even "best wishes, you sound like a nice person."

"He" was a nonexistent fake, possibly orchestrated by an overseas organized crime syndicate. I quickly learned that Ax Murderer #4 is what is called a catfisher—not even a real-if-dysfunctional man like Ax Murderer #3. Heck, Ax Murderer #4 wasn't even an ax murderer, as hideous as that would be. Was this worse?

Our generation of women grew up trusting people for the most part, and this new requirement of understanding photographic skullduggery is suddenly a critical and not-yet-developed skill. We would be more skeptical in the future.

Deeply shook, but sadder and wiser, the next day I went back to the pool with my girlfriends. Negativity ruled my thoughts. *Perhaps I should just give up on dating and enjoy life with my friends. If I keep my social calendar full, I won't feel so alone all the time. Why do I even bother with these stupid dating sites?* I was low, lower than a snake's belly as they say in Arizona.

Thankfully, the Washed-Up Cheerleaders and the Homecoming Queen didn't let that last. We returned to gab and laughs and fun in the sun and at some point, it was suggested that I try a different dating site called OurTime, targeted to over-fifties looking for real relationships.

Hmm . . . might be worth a try. I'd been knocked face-flat into the Arizona dust, but I was going to get up and try again.

And it seemed to work, because it was on that site that I would meet Dave Ax Murderer #5.

May through June 2024

## Here, There, Everywhere an Ax Murderer

I refused to quit. I would keep looking for love, for a real relationship, if it killed me. Luckily, it hadn't yet.

On the OurTime dating site, things seemed to be looking up. I'd connected over text and then quickly on the phone with a fun, funny, charming man, Dave Ax Murderer #5. While I was still in Arizona—though sadly the Washed-Up Cheerleaders and the Homecoming Queen had had to depart for their own homes—Dave Ax Murderer #5 and I spent several phone conversations laughing about the ridiculous online dating stories everyone seems to have. On a more somber note, both of his parents had recently passed, and we bonded over grief stories too. I began to feel connection.

But we hadn't met in person yet, and meanwhile another potential match pinged on my phone: Steve Ax Murderer #6. Over text and phone, Steve and I chatted amiably. We got along great, right away. Early on in our conversations, I asked him to send photos of himself with his buddies. (When a person isn't real, he can't send a photo of himself with his friends.)

Steve responded with four photos, three of them with golf friends, one with his daughter in front of Fenway Park. We had baseball in common! This could be fun. Steve was tall with an athletic build; my eyes lit up, seeing pickleball potential. Most important, his profile said Christian. I was getting excited.

I would fly from Arizona to Seattle in a few days and was already planning to stay at my younger son's home in the Seattle suburbs for a while. Steve asked, why not join him for a game of golf in nearby Mukilteo while I was so near to Seattle?

Why not, indeed? I wasn't sure my golf game would be too impressive, but I wasn't going to let that stop me. It'd been two years since I'd swung a club at Birch Bay Village Golf Club with Bob and our dear friends Doug and Sandy Thomas, but golf is like riding a bike, isn't it? Isn't it?! I hoped so.

Three days until I fly to Washington for our golf date. I relax on the back patio of my Arizona home, a tall glass of ice water on the table before me, enjoying the view of the midafternoon sun lighting up the jagged horizon of distant mountains. I lean back, close my eyes for a moment, feel that heavenly sunshine. Hmm . . . let's see . . . what photo of me should I send Steve? Something that tells him about me, about my cherished family, about what is dear to me . . . a photo that tells him I am real and alive and seeking authentic connection. A truthful photo.

Ah! I know just the one. I open my photos app, scroll back a couple of weeks. Here it is! In the photo, I'm with grandchildren Logan and Zoey at Birch Bay State Park. We are all three on bikes, feet on the ground, smiling, about to head out riding on the wide paved path near the curving bay. The photo captures the beauty of the park in the summer with the log-strewn sandy beach, the gleaming bay, the fringe of magnificent trees on the far shore.

Here on my patio in Arizona, looking at the photo, I smile, remembering that moment. This is just right. This will do nicely.

Tap. Send. The photo flies over the internet into Steve's phone. Immediately, I get his response.

"Nice boobs."

*What? What?!* My smile vanishes. My upbeat mood evaporates like a raindrop in the desert. Hopeful anticipation whooshes out of my lungs like air from a bike tire going flat, like a golf club missing the ball on the tee, swishing through nothingness.

I text back. "Are you drunk?"

His answer: "Maybe a little?"

There is only one answer I can send. I do not hesitate. "Best wishes." I am too deflated to even add the standard "You seem like a nice person." Because I am honest and frankly, he no longer seems like a nice person.

Then I delete Steve Ax Murderer #6.

June 2024

# The Best Day

I will not quit. I will try again. No knight on a white horse has yet ridden up my driveway in Arizona or Washington, so I must.

Speaking of those two states, my body was rebelling against my last five months' travel schedule of flitting back and forth from Southwest hot-dry to Pacific Northwest cold-wet—not to mention the debilitating grief I was battling. Before the Horrendous Event, I never had nosebleeds, but now I was getting them frequently. My nose would inexplicably start to gush at inopportune times when driving or sleeping. I wasn't sure what to do about that.

Meanwhile, on an up note, I am still chatting via text and phone with Dave Ax Murderer #5. He lives on Whidbey Island, forty-five minutes' drive from Bellingham. I tell him, upfront and point-blank, I'm not looking for a hookup but a genuine, lasting relationship. I share the "nice boobs" story, saying it's baffling how anyone could think that would land well. Dave Ax Murderer #5 assures me he is a gentleman who's seeking a real relationship.

He invites me to meet him for lunch and a walk around the charming waterside town of La Conner.

Starting from Bellingham, I leave early. I would be driving past the crash site on Highway 20 where Bob died, and I want to visit.

I know exactly where it is. I pull off the road, take a blanket, trek to the makeshift memorial others have made with its white cross and photo of Bob. I lay down on my blanket and cry, for the life he lost, for our life together that is no more. I cry because that is what you do when the love you cherish is killed in an intersection by a drug-user fleeing police.

Then I pull myself together and drive to the attractive little town of La Conner, parking on the main street.

It's a beautiful, sunny day in early June, with puffy white clouds scudding overhead and a breeze off the water. I've dressed with care, in my white denim jacket, lightweight sweater underneath, capri-length pants, sandals I can walk in. I see him waiting for me a couple of doors down. Oh! Dave Ax Murderer #5 is dashing, handsome, smiling. Our first in-person meeting holds no awkwardness; we move easily into conversation, picking up from our last phone call. We wander the long street, check out restaurant menus posted in vintage storefront windows, pick one, settle in a cozy booth wrapped with bead-board paneling and a lantern overhead.

Lunch is full of laughter, stories, even tears, since both his parents have died in the previous five months. But mostly we laugh about dating stories and anything else we can think of to possibly laugh at. After three hours, we depart the restaurant to wander artsy gift shops, stroll the waterfront, sit on a bench, watch the boats float by, talk more.

What's this, what's this? My nose! I feel a trickle down my upper lip and swipe it with the sleeve of my white jacket. Oh no! This is not just a runny nose but a massive, gushing bleed. I know from previous conversation that Dave Ax Murderer #5 hates blood; hearing that was reassuring at the time because what kind of ax murderer hates blood?

"I'm sorry, this is awful, how's this for a first impression?" I babble, swiping my sleeve at my nose again, further streaking the white denim. I feel like a fourteen-year-old getting her period on a first date. "I'll be right back." I run to the public bathroom, clean up what I can, stanch the bloody nose, return to the bench with what decorum I can muster—and find that my bleeding nose doesn't matter. With this engaging, charming, fun and funny guy, we keep talking, keep laughing.

Because it's going well, because this has real potential, I need to broach the one item in our dating website profiles that does not completely align. I'd checked the box Christian/Protestant. He'd checked Spiritual/Not Religious.

His hand is on my knee. I lay my hand atop his, swallow, speak gently. "Dave, you've talked about growing up in a Christian family. I am Christian, you are spiritual. Might there be some overlap? Is there commonality between us? Could we find it?"

And Dave, credit to him, is truthful. He does not believe in God. He doesn't believe in Heaven. No, he will never change his mind.

Unbidden tears spring to my eyes, then to his, as I speak candidly from my heart, from the rock-solid belief at my core. "Honestly Dave, I could see us perhaps in a great long-term relationship, meaning marriage, but in the upcoming years, one of us is going to die first. When I am totally in love with you, and if you were to die first, I would not be okay. I would not know where you were. If you don't believe in Heaven, how would you be there?"

Now, after hours of nonstop chatter, we are silent.

I know this had to be said. I am a straight shooter, I know what I want, and it's a courtesy to others to not beat around the bush, even on a first date.

We get up from the bench. It's over. It's never going to work. Dave Ax Murderer #5 walks me to my car, opens my door, nods and smiles, a sad smile.

He closes the door, and I drive away.

June/July 2024

# The Kiss

As it turns out, romantic attraction is not so easily turned off. I could not stop thinking about Dave Ax Murderer #5, the handsome and appealing non-Christian who would never work. No matter what I was doing, thoughts of him, of his funny stories and endearing glances, pushed their way into my head. My mind seemed untethered from my will. My will said, *You know it will never work, forget about him, move on*. And then my mind romped free like a dog off leash, running right back to him.

What *is* this? What happened to the standard, "best wishes, you seem like a nice person?" His mother's funeral is this week; maybe I'm meant to be praying for him. But nothing worked, and finally, unable to stand the firestorm in my head, I texted him. "Is it normal to meet someone for four hours and then think about them nonstop for three days?"

We were soon on the phone, him reminding me that he'd bought lunch last time, with the cute deal of "you buy next time." Theoretically, I owed him lunch. We put a date on the calendar, a couple of weeks hence since both our calendars were full.

Meanwhile, regular life ensued.

On Father's Day, en route to my younger son Tory's home in the Seattle suburbs, I swing by Whidbey Island to check out a gift shop a friend had recommended. On this blustery, rainy day, I spend more than a few minutes in the warm, inviting store. I see an artisan-made compass rose with a brass metal compass set in polished walnut. It's pretty cool. Dave Ax Murderer #5 has told me he lives on Whidbey Island overlooking the water, facing southwest. This will be a perfect gift. I buy it. I'll give it to him at our future lunch date.

I glance at my watch. Still too early to go to Tory's. Back in my car, I google "fun things Whidbey Island." There is a public beach nearby. I drive to it, park in the gravel lot, stroll through thigh-high beach grass to the water's edge. I walk east into the wind and cold, head down, musing about Father's Day, thinking about Bob, praying for my boys and their families. These special days, meant for gathering, laden with memory, are hard on all of us.

Enough of that. Time to go. It's spitting rain now, just a light, passing shower. I turn and trek back through the drizzle to the parking lot. And there, I see what I had not seen the first time: near the beach, just past the public property line, is a two-story house. I freeze, dumbfounded. The second story has a black railing encircling a balcony. It is the balcony and railing on which Dave Ax Murderer #5 had taken his profile photo for the OurTime dating website. I am standing next to his home. My car is parked two hundred feet from his front door.

What are the chances? My friend and housemate Courtney's saying flashes through my mind: You can't make this stuff up! Nor can I make up what comes next, because I do what any sane stalker would do. I drop to my hands and knees on the sand, then flop down flat on my belly and army-crawl through the beach grass toward my car.

Hitch forward, pull my legs behind me, hitch forward, pull legs behind. I'm getting seriously sandy but I'm making itchy, scratchy progress. I dearly hope there is no snake in the grass. Are there snakes on Washington beaches? I don't know. I start to giggle. Hitch, pull, hitch, pull. I glance back toward the balcony. No one there, thank goodness. My giggles become laughter. I used to be normal, I really did. Hitch, pull. My laughter bubbles up uncontrollably now, maniacally. Hitch, pull, hitch, pull. Oh no, here comes a family: dad, mom, two small sons, walking from parking lot to beach, arms loaded with soccer ball, blanket, a big plastic bat and wiffle ball.

The young mother looks down at me with alarm. "Are you okay?"

I pause, lift my head from the sand, look at them, think. There is no way to preserve dignity when you are lying belly down on wet sand, hiding in the grass. I think, *I don't know. Am I okay? Or have I turned into a stalker?*

"I'm fine, gotta go!" I roll to my feet, stand up, brush my front, sprint to my car, start it up. I turn my head to back the car out and thus I see, coming up the beach in front of that house, a middle-aged man and a little girl, holding hands. It's Dave Ax Murderer #5 and his granddaughter.

Oh gosh. I slump down in the driver's seat as much as possible while still seeing over the steering wheel to drive, and hightail it out of there.

Two weeks later, Dave Ax Murderer #5 and I meet for our second lunch date at a restaurant on Whidbey Island. I have a card to go with my gift of the compass rose. My written words, "Thanks for showing me there are normal people on dating sites.

I hope we each find our true north" are heartfelt if mushy. He tears up. I do too.

Once again, lunch stretches over hours as we talk and laugh (I see no need to share the story of my accidental stalking). We clearly have an emotional connection and enjoy each other's company. We speak again of our different views on religion. I ask if we could be friends without benefits. He replies that it would be a challenge, but he's willing to try.

"Martha, come see my house," he says finally, dabbing his mouth with a napkin. "You'll love the sea view, and the garden is extensive." Over the past weeks, he's talked so often about his garden. I *would* like to see it. (Properly this time, not glancing wildly over my shoulder while army-crawling through beach grass.)

I gather my sweater and purse, smile at him, stand up. "Okay, thank you, I'll drive over after you. But just to be clear," I stop and look at him, for emphasis, "I'm not coming to your house for sex."

Dave laughs as he holds open the restaurant door for me. "Of course. I'm a gentleman, you know that."

We tour the house and the gardens, which are as beautiful as advertised. The yard, the house, the waterfront, him—all lovely.

We sit on his deck overlooking the water, watching eagles wheel and dive overhead. I think of a nature documentary I saw recently where an eagle swooped down to nab a tasty fish, caught it, and labored upward, the fish wriggling desperately in those claws. No! I push that thought away, but now my disobedient mind strays to something Dave Ax Murderer #5 told me weeks ago about his gun collection. I think, *Hmm . . . I hardly know this man, we are sitting only a few yards from his twenty-two guns, and even though those guns are locked away, I could end up on an episode of* Dateline, *that true-crime television show* . . . whoa. I put the brakes on that too. Those thoughts are fit only for a story to tell the Washed-Up Cheerleaders and the Homecoming Queen. I don't need them in my head now.

I bring myself back to this pleasant moment on this deck. Our conversation lulls. Then Dave stands, leans over me, bends down, and gives me a most passionate kiss.

I have not been kissed in twenty-one months. I start to shake. I can hardly breathe. My last kiss was from my beloved husband, right before he left for a ride, a few hours before he would be killed. My system is suddenly and dangerously overloaded with emotions, of memories of Bob, of our love that lasted thirty-eight years, of how near-impossible it might be for me to ever be in love with someone else.

I know what is happening, what will happen.

"I have to go, I'm sorry, I can't do this or anything else," I say, bumbling toward the front door, finding my shoes, trying to remember how to tie a shoe. I back away, babbling. "I'm not what you want at all. I just need to go." I flee the house, the yard, the gardens. I flee like Joseph fled from Potiphar's wife in the Book of Genesis. Joseph ran from her attempted seduction, a seduction that he knew would seal his doom in Heaven and on Earth. I get into my car—a blessing that Joseph did not have—and drive away and I don't stop shaking until I pass the little city of Burlington.

I make it home. I text Dave Ax Murderer #5: "Arrived safely." I add, "Best wishes, you are such a great person. But we both know this isn't going to work."

He agrees and wishes me well.

July 22, 2024

# Brain Chemistry and Other Mysteries

The early morning sun warms my shoulders as the temperature nudges up toward seventy. It's nearly 9:00 a.m. I straighten up from pulling weeds in my front yard, rubbing my back. Stephanie, my daughter-in-law, will be here any minute to drop off the two grandkids to spend the day with me.

How will we three spend this lovely summer day? Maybe grab beach towels, drape them over our shoulders, and pad in flip-flops down the asphalt lane to Lake Whatcom's swimming beach? Or ride bikes through the neighborhood? Or just hang here, play UNO, and hit wiffle balls in the backyard. Maybe (sinister laugh) I can get the kids to help me in the yard and pay them big bucks. That's worked once before. Perhaps we can get something accomplished, like picking up all the leathery laurel leaves that have fallen all over the backyard.

But Zoey and Logan, two of the most gorgeous children ever born (no way am I biased) leap out of the car with food on their minds. Zoey, six years old now, with her soft brown wispy hair and shining brown eyes, is waving a kids' cookbook that I gave her and talking a mile a minute. "French toast, Nana? Can we make French toast?"

Logan, nine years old with short, thick jet-black hair and deep green eyes, is a perfect combination of his dashing dad and exotically beautiful mom. He's my little one who's not so little anymore. He gives me a quick hug and rockets past me into the family room, keen to get back to his iPad.

I call after him. "Okay, Logan, you can finish that game."

Logan is engaging and athletic when we can get the screen off. I admit to resorting to terrorist negotiation tactics with him occasionally, such as, "If you do this, then we can do this." I might say, "if you play outside with us for an hour, we can have ice cream; if you help me in the yard for a while, you can have screen time." With all my experience managing grandchildren, I consider myself a highly trained negotiator. I think I may have a future with the FBI or possibly Interpol.

Zoey's in the kitchen now, up on a kitchen stool next to the counter singing a little scrap of a song, cracking eggs into the batter like a home ec teacher, stirring like a pro, not slopping a bit over the edge of the bowl.

And then it hits me. Unrelenting tears from me, tears that won't stop. Zoey looks up in alarm, an eggshell in her small hand. My tears flow faster, my breath goes ragged, I'm snuffling now in a desperate attempt to stop crying. I must stop, yet I can't stop. This is ridiculous! I cannot cry in front of a child.

Darling Zoey, with her philosophical personality, knows just what to say, things I've said to her and her brother for months.

"Don't be sad, Nana, we still have each other!"

Tears roll from my eyes as I struggle to get hold of myself. What is upsetting me on this normal day in a normal week of a lovely sunny summer in Bellingham?

Zoey, still on the stool, drops the eggshell to hug me around the middle. Her eyes grow wider as she looks at me. "Nana, don't be sad, we still have the rest of our family and they all love us."

Logan, having heard me crying, sprints in from the family room and swivels his head from Zoey to me in confusion. I take a deep, shuddering breath. I must not upset these darling children, these precious children who've also had a traumatic year with the death of their adored PapaBob.

Why can't I stop? What trigger is sending me over the cliff today? My emotions are whirling out of control and I don't even know why.

Zoey is still talking, tilting her head to one side, nodding a little, still trying to comfort me. "PapaBob is in Heaven, we will see him again and we will all be happy there."

I am further undone, if that's possible, by this emotional intelligence coming from a six-year-old.

"Nana, Nana, are you okay?" Logan's oft-mischievous face now matches his sister's for alarm.

"Yes, yes, I'm okay," I lie, grabbing a kitchen towel and snuffling into it. One deep breath, then another, and with herculean effort, my tears abate for a moment. I lean down to a lower cabinet to get the electric griddle, hiding my face. "Let's fry that French toast."

That morning, we ate French toast with butter and syrup, and my tears flowed between bites. We played hide 'n seek throughout the big house, and my tears flowed whether I was hiding or seeking. We played UNO, sitting cross-legged on the family room carpet, and my tears flowed, and not because I was losing the card game again.

After an hour and a half of tears streaming down my face for no apparent reason, I walk out onto our front deck and phone my doctor's office.

"My husband died twenty months ago. I'm having a really hard time. Could someone see me today?"

"Yes, at 4:00 p.m." The receptionist's voice is filled with concern.

Whew, I think, thank you, because two weeks from Friday is not going to work for me.

About an hour later they called back, requesting I come in immediately.

"Wait, what? I can't, I have my grandkids here. But 4:00 p.m. will be fine."

"Oh," the receptionist said, "we understood your husband died twenty minutes ago and you needed help immediately."

"No, twenty months ago! I've been somewhat stabilized until today. I can make it till four. See you then."

Ah, the magic of modern medicine. Apparently, antidepressants lower the bar on everything that happens in your brain: The good is less euphoric, the bad less devastating. With meds, I soon discovered that all of life feels "less." Less energy, less engagement, less motivation.

I soon found I couldn't live like that; I needed the high of that great pickleball hit. (Okay, that doesn't happen often but when it does, whee! Endorphins!) This prescription for antidepressants made me want to sleep, but I'd awaken even after a three-hour nap still fatigued, drained, and fuzzy-minded. I stopped taking the pills and haven't had a relapse—yet—of unstoppable tears in front of someone.

Trust me, I still have the pills and I'm not afraid to use them. Grief is hard and profoundly tiring. As my doctor said, grief exhausts your brain chemistry. I'd tell anyone, don't hesitate to get medical help.

A few days later, I was telling my wise friend Susan about my meltdown. In her intuitive Susan way, she asked what happened during the days before my meltdown. Who was I with? What feelings was I stuffing down inside? Susan is aware of my Oscar-worthy actress abilities when I shove grief down deep and act like everything is normal.

And then it struck me. I knew the trigger. Recently, two people who are somewhat new in my life had each said, at different times, "Oh, he died on his motorcycle."

They'd spoken dismissively, in passing. They hadn't intended for it to land the way it did, but this is what my subconscious heard: "Bob was dumb to ride a motorcycle. Of course, he died and it's all his fault. He doesn't care how much pain you're in. He's happy to be dead. He was riding his motorcycle on purpose and these last twenty months of living hell are your problem now. And nobody even feels sorry for you, because you know that anyone who rides a motorcycle is stupid and probably deserves to die."

So, there it is. The subconscious triggers, the things that you don't realize some part of your mind is telling you, the things that will make you break. Those thoughts were roiling deep down like magma beneath a dormant volcano, and they manifested as floods of tears on that sunny summer day making French toast and playing UNO with the grandkids.

Our hearts are the source of all our thoughts, beliefs, and actions. Take care what thoughts you allow yourself. As it says in Proverbs 4:23: "Guard your heart with all diligence, for from it flow the springs of life."

Be careful of the narrative you tell yourself. It matters.

Summer 2024

## Is This *The Jerry Springer Show*?

At home in Bellingham, washing dishes at my kitchen sink, I glance out the window over my sloping driveway. No knight in shining armor riding a white steed has yet cantered through our leafy neighborhood and up my driveway to rescue me. For a moment, holding a soapy pan under warm spray, I picture this mythical knight waving to astonished neighbors as he rides past on his way to find me. I rinse the pan, turn it upside down on the drainboard. No knight yet. It seems I'll have to keep trying to meet people, in person and online.

Lately, I have been chatting online with a new guy, Ax Murderer #7. He seems nice, and his photo with friends shows he's real. He's a grandfather who lives in the Seattle area, not far from some of my extended family. I'd like to visit my relatives anyway, so I accept Ax Murderer #7's offer to meet in a café near their house for breakfast.

When the day comes, once again I greet the "match" at a restaurant, he opens the door for me, we settle into a booth. His face is creased with smile lines and framed with curly steel-colored hair. He has blue eyes, those rare blue eyes that sparkle. We chat, peruse the menus, order, talk. He seems nice, normal. He's been divorced for quite a while.

"Yeah, my ex-wife was an alcoholic," he says, settling back against the pleather seat. "It was hard on our kids. One Christmas Eve she came home smashed, stumbled against the Christmas tree, and it toppled over on her. Next morning, the kids raced downstairs early. They found their mom lying there, foul and snoring in a tangle of tinsel."

Taken aback, I stay silent. My eyes widen when he tells me she was so nuts, she was actually on an episode of *The Jerry Springer Show*.

"The kids were scared of her, and more scared of the men she brought home," he says. "She got mixed up with some brutal characters, dealers, who got her on cocaine first, then heroin. Of course, it didn't happen all at once, and during the times she was clean, she was fine with the kids. She's their mom after all. They loved her—until she'd fall off the wagon and come after them again."

I wish I could put my fingers in my ears. A wave of sorrow washes over me, for Ax Murderer #7 with his twinkling eyes, for his traumatized children, now grown, even for his wayward ex.

It is all too much for me. I end it gently as we depart the restaurant. "Best wishes, you seem like a nice person."

Two more long-texting, seemingly nice people follow, Ax Murderers #8 and then #9, who turn out to be professional scammers. Even after you recognize them as catfishers, you never know who or what is behind them: sick individuals or organized crime? Luckily, I figure out they are fakes before any damage is done.

During this time, I have more than one pep talk with my friend, the one who after many tries met the man online who is now her husband. Maybe I'll find someone too. But Bob had been

The One for me. Who could replace him? A mythical knight on a white horse? Could online dating ever produce this man?

I try not to compare today's online dating with the way I met Bob, which was as far from *The Jerry Springer Show* as you can get. It was late August 1981 when we were introduced by his friends Doug and Cara Forhan at the state softball tournament held at Frank Geri Fields in Bellingham that year. (Of course, Bob and I met at a softball game. That foreshadowed our lifelong love of baseball.) It took Bob two weeks to muster the nerve to call and ask me out.

Bob, not quite four years older than I, had graduated from Washington State University in Pullman, Washington, with an accounting degree. He was working in Bellingham then, trying to figure out what to do with an accounting degree while not becoming an accountant.

I was a junior at Western Washington University in Bellingham, majoring in Secondary Education Home Economics, living in a college apartment I shared with three other gals. I remember the evening he came to pick me up for our first date.

I open the apartment door and see Bob with his summer tan, freshly shaved. He's twenty-three years old. We're going to dinner followed by a football game, so he's wearing good jeans with a new-looking flannel shirt and clean athletic shoes, carrying a down vest for when the evening gets cooler. But all that is on the periphery of my consciousness, because when I see Bob standing there, smiling nervously, I hear a voice in my head, saying "this is who I will marry." A sharp intake of breath from me, a sense of puzzle pieces tumbling into place, an other-worldly feeling that I had not felt before, or since. It is a wild sensation, as if the voice of God is speaking.

After that first date, he'd pick me up after he got off work, after my late class at the iconic, ivy-draped Old Main building at WWU. We'd go out for dinner or he'd come to the apartment I shared with the other girls where I'd whip up something for him and anybody else who happened to be on hand for dinner.

We were real people interacting in real time in the real world. Like everyone else, we were blissfully unaware of any other way. We'd never heard of catfishers, but if we had, we would have imagined it involved a cat hunting by a stream.

We were married in June 1984.

Now, twenty-two months after his death, I try to choose happiness instead of loneliness, try to rock Option B. I have taped to my bathroom mirror a card given me by the LifeNet Health organ donation folks the night Bob died when our home was a chaos of state troopers and support officers and tears and trauma and shock. I signed a document then allowing donation of his corneas so someone else could use them to see the people they love.

That night, I couldn't appreciate the words on that LifeNet Health card, but I do now: "It can happen, as it does with all living things, that people become ill or get hurt. Mostly they get better, but there are times when they are so hurt or so ill that they die. It is sad, but that is how it is for people. It is their lifetime. No matter how long or short, lifetimes are really all the same. They have beginnings, and endings, and living in between."

Every morning when I read that, I focus on the great times of living, the "in between." I choose to be happy about the blessed and beautiful life we had, starting with the evening he came to my door, smiling nervously, to take me out to the ballgame.

Late Summer 2024

## He Is Kryptonite

I think yardwork may be the end of me, or at least the end of my back. This is another thing about widowhood: All the work your husband did around the house you now get to do, and there's more of it than you ever realized.

I straighten up, one gloved hand rubbing my lower back, the other holding my shovel. I am at home in Bellingham, shoveling bark mulch onto foundation beds around the house. It's Saturday afternoon and raining, but not hard enough to keep me indoors. (In the Pacific Northwest, it takes a Biblical deluge worthy of Noah to keep you inside.)

I lean on my shovel, taking in the view that includes a stretch of Lake Whatcom. It won't hurt to rest a minute. This week has been busy, with friends, grandkids, pickleball, sewing group. I keep my calendar full, so I don't dwell on my future where the choice sometimes seems to be loneliness or the company of a dysfunctional true-crime talk-show candidate.

But—I have met Bob Ax Murderer #10, a retired tugboat captain and a captain of commercial fishing vessels who is currently on a boat in Alaska. Thinking of him cheers me. He holds potential.

I'm back shoveling bark when my phone pings. Oh, good, something from Bob Ax Murderer #10. He can't always get a signal. I drop my shovel immediately.

But it's not Bob Ax Murderer #10. It's a text from Dave Ax Murderer #5, the one from whom I fled after that Academy Award-winning kiss on his deck five weeks ago. Yes, *that* Dave, my favorite lunch date, the hilarious conversationalist, emotionally intelligent, dashingly handsome one.

I see his text: "How is dating going for you?"

I think, *What? What the heck?*

I abandon the shoveling, go in out of the rain, and talk on the phone with Dave Ax Murderer #5 for a half-hour. My schedule, like his, is open this evening. We agree to meet in La Conner for dinner in our "friends without benefits" situation.

Perfect! I shower and dress, happy and excited about my date. I enjoy his company so much and he seems to enjoy mine.

I drive to La Conner. I don't even cry going past the crash site. Instead, I smile and wave, and hope my cherished, departed husband is happy that I'm trying to be happy again. I'm pretty high on the sparkle spectrum tonight. I smile, thinking of my friend and former housemate Courtney who coined "sparkle spectrum" and who helped me so much.

Dave Ax Murderer #5 and I settle into a booth at the Oyster & Thistle, an inviting place serving food grown in the Skagit Valley or caught in local waters. I have a chilled pinot grigio, he has bourbon on the rocks. Once again, we feel instant companionship. He says he can tell I am doing better. He apologizes for kissing me without permission on his deck five weeks ago. He apologizes for misreading my signals that day. He apologizes for spooking me.

I explain that my fight-or-flight response was triggered by memories of kissing only Bob for decades, and by the shock of kissing someone new. When I say that I hadn't been kissed since Bob's death, Dave Ax Murderer #5 is gobsmacked. (Of course I hadn't kissed anyone. I wouldn't get physical with anyone I was trying to date. I know, what a novel concept! But I seek love and commitment.)

He reaches across the table to hold my hand. He affirms kindly, "I bet that kiss was upsetting for you, since your last kiss was from your husband."

The candlelight on the table is flickering. The wine is fine. The restaurant, cozy and welcoming, hums around us. I enjoy his company so much. I leave my hand in his.

He says, "Come to my house?"

Oh! No. No. Gently but firmly, no.

He walks me to my car, and kisses me lusciously, passionately. He is my Kryptonite—Kryptonite as in an extraordinary, exploitable weakness, like Achilles' heel but more so. I know I must keep my distance or this will end badly. He is not the right guy for me. I am not the right girl for him.

I extricate myself, drive home through the lovely lingering evening light, through the farmlands of the Skagit Valley, past the crash site again, where I repeat, *Bob is in a better place, so much better he wouldn't want to come back even if he could.* Nearly two years after his death, these are thoughts I conjure still to soothe my soul.

I get home and get into bed, still giggling about some of the conversations that Dave Ax Murderer #5 and I had tonight. I think about Dave: endearing, handsome, likable . . . lovable? I think, *if only we were on the same page about God, about Heaven.*

I snuggle under a blanket, look out the big window as the summer twilight darkens to navy-blue. *Dave kind of looks like Bob. He's fun and funny like Bob. He's a people person, like Bob. If only we had the most important thing in common!*

Two days go by, filled again with friends and grandkids. I finish spreading the bark mulch. (My back survives.) On the second evening when my phone lights up with Dave Ax Murderer #5's phone call, we chat for twenty minutes about our individual plans for fall, about how he's settling his parents' estate, about the fun we had during our three long dates.

That's when he drops the bomb. "You know," he says, "we could get married."

I drop into a chair. Marriage. I have just received a proposal of marriage.

The conversation continues, and the idea develops. We talk about the places we might travel, the fun we could have with our grandchildren, the clear attraction we have for each other.

"I haven't stopped thinking about you since we met in June," Dave Ax Murderer #5 says. It's sweet and appealing and mutual.

And then, the defining moment. "We could have an open marriage," he says.

How would "open marriage" even make sense to me, a person who seeks nothing but love and commitment? My mind spins: He's wondering whether I'd consider an open marriage!? I'm wondering what I'm doing chatting with this lunatic. I think of Courtney's other phrase: *You can't make this stuff up!* A phrase that has gotten way more use than I had ever imagined.

Goodbye Dave Ax Murderer #5, for good this time. Goodbye, Kryptonite.

I bring up his contact on my phone and tap, "Delete."

But this story has a coda, a last gasp of *you can't make this stuff up*, a final mention even after he was pulled off stage and the curtain fell.

Weeks later in Arizona, I was dining out with Phoenix friends who were hosting a Bellingham friend I'd known since our growing-up days. I was regaling them with dating stories, including Dave Ax Murderer #5. The next morning, I sent that Bellingham friend a photo of Dave.

Her response? "Oh my gosh, I know him! I worked with him for years at a company in Burlington. He is fun, with a heart of gold, but man alive, is he a flirt! And absolutely not marriage material."

Yes. I know.

August 2024

# Beauty and the Beast

Who departs the Pacific Northwest during the lovely cool summer for the soaring heat of Arizona in August? Anyone in their right mind can look at a weather app and see record-breaking temperatures in the Southwest. Who does that? Two people who might fall in love.

With Dave Ax Murderer #5 out of the picture, it was natural for Bob Ax Murderer #10, a retired tugboat captain currently on a fishing vessel in Alaska, to come to the fore.

The first puzzle was how the OurTime dating website matched us in the first place. I had listed my home as Bellingham and my dating parameters as seventy-five miles from that epicenter. Bob 2.0 (as I was calling him) had listed his home as Florence, Arizona. That's less than thirty miles from my winter home in Queen Creek, Arizona, but the OurTime site didn't know I had a home there. Bob 2.0 used to live and work in Bellingham, but the OurTime site didn't know that either.

While he was in Alaska and I in Bellingham, and before we met in person, we spent hours during the long summer evenings on the phone. After ten days of this, we decided to meet in person. He could fly from Alaska to his home in Florence, and I'd fly from Bellingham to my home in Queen Creek. In Arizona, we were somewhat close geographically. Who knew? We could have daytime dates there. How easy was that? Plus, since we each had our own place, there'd be no "friends with benefits" concerns, which is one road I would never get on. What I want is to be married again someday, and I never hesitated to make that clear.

Since Bob 2.0 is a gentleman, this made sense to him too. We made plans to swap the gorgeous weather of the Pacific Northwest and southeast Alaska for the swelter of Arizona. During our last phone call before the meet-up, I ask him for his last name.

"Tray," Bob 2.0 says, then spells "T R A Y."

I laugh a little and say, "Oh! My last name is Bray, B R A Y."

He gasps. "Seriously, Bray with a B?"

"Yes . . . ?" I pause, a question in my voice.

"You aren't going to believe this!" he says. "I need to tell you something, but I'm afraid it'll upset you."

"What?" I say lightly. "What could upset me?"

Long pause from Bob 2.0.

I wait.

"It all makes sense to me now," he says. "But it's . . . kind of awful."

Now I *am* concerned. "Tell me quick," I say.

"Okay," he begins. "Here goes. In late September 2022, I was at the Coast Guard station in Bellingham renewing certifications for my captain licenses."

That date. September 2022. When Bob died. Just the mention of that date causes pain to flood through me.

He continues. "After I finished the paperwork at the station, I wandered over to the net house—you know, where the fishermen store those miles of nets—to see if I'd run into any old pals. Sure enough I did, but they were shocked to see me. They ran over to me, yelling 'Bob, what are you doing here? We heard on the radio that you died yesterday in a motorcycle accident in Anacortes!' Some of them even hugged me. Whoa. I had no idea what they were talking about."

He carries on with the story. "Everybody was talking at once. It took a while for me to understand: A local Bellingham guy with a name almost exactly like mine had died in a horrible accident the day before, and my pals down at the waterfront thought it was me. Bray, Tray . . . on the radio it sounded the same."

I am struck dumb, clutching my phone.

Bob 2.0's voice grows gentle. "Now, here I am, speaking with his widow, making plans to meet her."

Once again, that saying springs to mind. *You can't make this stuff up!*

The thought of meeting Bob 2.0 in person sends me right up and off the sparkle spectrum. Let's see if the connection we feel on the phone holds up in person! I slip into a pleasant daydream, thinking of our phone conversations. Bob 2.0 is appealing, interesting, kind. My euphoria lasts through the flight, the landing at Phoenix-Mesa Gateway Airport, the transfer to my home in Queen Creek—where it's suddenly replaced by an anxiety meltdown. *What if he isn't real? What if this is a cruel joke? What if he doesn't come?*

It's Sunday afternoon. He's supposed to fly from Ketchikan to Mesa tomorrow. *What if he never shows up? What if I've been catfished again and here I am in 112-degree heat, waiting to meet a person who isn't real?*

I'm tormented by a stew of boiling, roiling negativity, stirred up courtesy of the last two catfishers. This will never do. I take a deep breath and tap out a text to Bob 2.0.

"Sorry to bother you," my text begins. "I know you're wrapping up the boat, getting ready to leave. Can you shoot me a photo of yourself taken today? I feel you are too good to be true and I need to know you are real."

Within moments, I see his response: a picture of him on a dock in Alaska with a big fishing vessel behind him. He is darling! Thank you, Bob 2.0! Then he sends a photo of his face with a time stamp on his computer in the background. *Thank goodness. He is real, he is in real time, and he will soon be on his way to Arizona to meet me.*

My anxiety vanishes in a puff of excitement and plans. First things first: I check into the spa at my resort community, have a facial (chin hairs gone, check) and a pedicure (feet pretty for sandals and swimming, check) and lose five pounds (not checked, oh well!).

Tuesday morning, Bob 2.0 meets me and my friends Lori and Tim Spink for coffee at the main clubhouse in my gated community. Lori and Tim are in protect-Martha mode and grill Bob 2.0 with every imaginable question. Bob 2.0, unfazed, answers amiably, sometimes humorously, and soon he and Tim are cracking up like old friends. With that exam passed, our visit clicks into gear. We two swim at my community's main pool, have a shady lunch poolside, drive to Florence for dinner with Bob's best friends. As laughter bubbles up around the restaurant table, I take a moment to look, really look at him as he's telling a hilarious story. Bob 2.0 is broad and strong, five feet eleven inches tall, with a darling mustache, beautiful kind eyes, a jovial laugh, and a "one of the guys" personality. Earlier, he told me he was "rough around the edges," and joked that he and I are like "Beauty and the Beast." I sip my pinot grigio and smile. Bob 2.0 is attractive, and the fact that he lives in a guys' world of tugboats and fishermen makes him more so. As a retired certified captain for a marine transport company, he's the real deal.

I know a few more things about Bob 2.0. When he's at home in Arizona, he likes to drive his Polaris RZR Trail, a two-seater off-road vehicle, through the rough and beautiful land. He volunteers weekly at a food pantry, and he meets friends for dinner every week.

On Wednesday, I drive seventeen miles south to his house and he proudly shows me around. He built this house himself on a large lot with a mountain view. He has a huge private pool in the backyard; I can imagine the view of sunrises from that spot. It's romantic and fun when we jump in his truck and drive to Salt River to see the wild horses there, then carry on to a nearby town to his favorite restaurant for lunch.

Thursday, temperatures soar. I laugh in disbelief at the thermometer: 115 degrees. Back to my pool, indoor movies, massages for two at the spa. Friday is a day apart for us as he deals with an air conditioner issue at his place; Saturday, we swim at his big pool (is it swimming? Or just floating like half-submerged logs?) Sunday, we meet at his church, listen to a thought-provoking sermon, have lunch and . . . Conversation.

Ah yes, the Conversation, as our days together draw to a close. We both have so much on our minds: Is this working? Are we falling in love? Uppermost for me is that I can't live in Florence. I speak plainly: Your house is beautiful, your pool fabulous, but the wider neighborhood is questionable, and Florence—unappealingly—is home to multiple state, federal, county, and private prisons. Yes, when I'm with you, I feel safe, but I don't feel safe or comfortable in Florence.

Again, I speak directly. Do you like my gated resort community? Does being in that beautiful neighborhood with so many activities—pools, pickleball, cards, book clubs, bocci, cornhole, whiskey club (seriously, what neighborhood has a whiskey club?!)—appeal to you?

Bob 2.0 doesn't say much and, anyway, we are out of time as he drives me to the airport to catch my flight to Bellingham. He is to fly back to Ketchikan the following day.

During the week since our parting, we text once. His silence speaks volumes.

Yep, I'm pretty sure this is over. A week later, I compose a heartfelt goodbye text, thanking him for being a gentleman, telling him how glad I am that we had time together. He does not reply.

We were—are—each cemented into our different social cultures like rocks set in stone. This is another facet of dating in later life: You are both sixty and set in your ways, not sixteen and malleable. By this time, you are who you are. You are no longer twenty with the story of who you will be yet to be written.

September 2024

## I Will Come and Find You

At last! I am meeting a new acquaintance for a coffee date who is not an Ax Murderer, whom I did not meet via a dating website. Instead, we met the charming, old-fashioned way, via introduction by a mutual friend.

He and I had made a friendly connection during our first coffee meet-up a couple of weeks previously as we spoke of the grief of losing our spouses and, on a lighter note, of our shared passion for pickleball. Except that in pickleball, I am an amateur and Glen, having won numerous gold medals in the sport, is known nationally. A retired engineer, he's helped develop new equipment and even has a paddle named after him. In the contacts on my phone, I list him as "Glen the Pickleball Rockstar."

Today, driving south on Interstate 5 toward our second coffee date in the Seattle suburb of Redmond, my spirits lift higher than even this gorgeous autumn day warrants. I'm in my dad's 2007 Honda Ridgeline pickup truck, with the radio blasting a Kenny Chesney country classic, the windows cracked open, and scraps of the bark mulch I'd been hauling earlier blowing out of the empty truck bed. Hands on the wheel, a little fresh air blowing through my hair, I'm excited about seeing Glen again.

I move the old pickup into the lane for Interstate 405 and veer east into uncharted territory toward Redmond—and find myself crawling in heavy traffic. Oh no. I can't be late! My upbeat mood zooms downward, like a pickleball serve straight into the net. I glance down at my phone to see the Mapquest feature fading and my phone battery almost dead. Oh no, oh no! Of course, Dad's old truck doesn't have GPS; in this vehicle, I rely on my phone.

Without electronics, I suddenly have no idea where I'm going. Who has paper maps anymore? I shut down the phone, saving the last shreds of battery for later—if there is a later. I know I'm somewhere on the east side of Lake Washington and so is Redmond, but greater Seattle is a sprawling, unfamiliar metropolis to me. Traffic is still crawling. I punch the button to snap off the radio, and the cars ahead of me come to complete stop. We are now virtually parked on I-405.

After our promising first "date," I'm going to miss out on my second meet-up with Glen the Pickleball Rockstar.

No! I'm not giving up. I'm guessing I must be near Redmond. Traffic starts moving, so I take a chance, exit the interstate, and soon, am meandering down wonky country roads, roads Kenny Chesney might've sung about in happier times. What's this up ahead? The Chateau Ste. Michelle winery. I know the brand, but I still don't know where I am. Woodinville . . . is that it? Not that I know where Woodinville is in relation to Redmond. And then, DETOUR, a bright orange sign. ROAD CLOSED.

I pull the pickup into a gravel parking lot, tap on my phone, and call up my last smidgen of battery to call Glen. He picks up right away.

"You're close, no worries," Glen says breezily. He's not upset at all about me being late. Hearing his relaxed tone makes my stress evaporate. Then he says, "I can just jump in my car and come and find you, if that'd be easier."

I will come and find you. That phrase. Granddaughter Zoey said it when she was drawing the Valentine's store in Heaven, explaining that PapaBob will come and find me there because he loves me and misses me. Hearing that same phrase from Glen the Pickleball Rockstar makes my heart skip a beat.

I realize this is what I want. This is what my heart craves, to be found. I want to be cared for and loved by a person on my team, in my corner, helping me through life. I don't know if this will ever happen. I don't know who it might be.

Perhaps it is what we all crave. To be found. It is reminiscent of being found by Jesus in a way that causes our heart to hear and understand the Gospel message for the first time. It all happens because we were found. It all happens because we knew we were lost, and we want to be found.

So, in reality I have already had the most important Person in the universe come and find me. Then I had my fabulous first husband find me. I look forward to him finding me again in Heaven. Now, in this new life, this Option B life, perhaps I will be found one more time? Or perhaps not, as it is not necessary. I have already been found. That is all that matters.

Now and April 2016

# Less Talking, More Doing, and True North

Nobody knows who will make it to retirement. Heck, nobody knows who will even make it to tomorrow. This became abundantly clear to me one weekend in 2016.

My husband Bob and I, with three other couples, great friends all, were spending that April 2016 weekend at a house in the mountains east of Seattle. Is there anything as welcome as spring in the Cascades after the wet, cold, dark winter? Soaking up sunshine, luxuriating in the growing warmth and lengthening days, we biked, hiked, cooked, and laughed.

Our laughter reached a peak on one gorgeous mountain drive with the four husbands in a top-down Jeep and the four wives in a sedan when both cars pulled off at a scenic overlook. The four men jumped out of the Jeep for a better view. And what happened? Other women at the overlook started instantly, shamelessly flirting with our dashing husbands. We wives, in the car behind them, laughed out loud as we rolled our eyes. Could those women not see the men's wedding rings? Maybe they didn't see us wives parked right behind the Jeep. Of course, our men loved the attention, and later that evening, we heard their macho claims of "Yeah, I still got it!" more than once.

Our laughter reached its valley on our last night together. Around the campfire with our closest friends, Bob shared news that he'd been diagnosed the week before with prostate cancer. The cancer was caught early, a treatment plan was underway, and his prognosis was good. But there it was: Nobody knows who'll make it to retirement, or even to tomorrow.

So began our Less Talking, More Doing Club. We all had vacation time from work; let's start using it! (Bob's treatment plan was ultimately successful.) Over the ensuing months and years, we hiked the Pacific Crest Trail out of Stehekin, Washington, a hamlet unreachable by road in the heart of the North Cascades, with pack horses carrying our gear for three days and nights. We rented a houseboat on Shushwap Lake in British Columbia (holding an impromptu dance party on the top deck), enjoying the kayaking, hiking, and boating to the floating restaurant. We flew to Britain and hiked a major portion of Hadrian's Wall. We flew to France and bicycled through the Valley of Kings. If we could think of it, if we could plan it, we could do it.

Today, two years after the Horrendous Event, with Bob gone (and, heartwrenchingly, one other vibrant, beloved member of our Less Talking, More Doing Club, lost at age sixty to brain cancer), I am glad we didn't put off the fun. We didn't wait to celebrate our friendship, to love our people, to laugh and joke and care for one another. We didn't wait to love.

Today, I won't wait to love again. With all the strength I can muster, day after day, I make myself choose happiness, I make myself find the good in my new life.

For thousands of years, navigators used stars to set their direction. In the northern hemisphere, if they could see the north star, they could navigate endless ocean. Before Bob's death, I too knew my direction. I was subconsciously aware of my true north. I could solve problems, ease pain, help others, navigate obstacles, make sense of the world.

Then, in the hideous screech of a motorcyclist evading police, my true north vanished. I could no longer make sense of my life, of anything. I mostly wanted to accidentally die. I wanted all decisions to be made by someone else. I was scared, irrational, and profoundly disoriented.

At the opening of this book, I wrote that Bob's sudden traumatic death hit our world like a meteor slamming into Earth, knocking the very planet off course. His death also delivered a knockout punch to my true north. (For a long time, how I wished that punch had actually knocked me unconscious.)

But gradually, I caught my breath. Gradually, I could remember the blessings of my old life with Bob and the blessings of my new life without him. Family and friends dealing with their own lives, their own grief, helped me find my true north again, meaning I could gradually align my thoughts and actions with my core beliefs. They prayed with me, laughed and cried with me, reminded me of the teachings of Jesus we held in common. Gradually, I saw that my true north was still there ahead of me, just obscured by widow fog.

I believe that if I control my inner thoughts, if I choose to be happy and thankful, it will become a habit that reinforces itself, and I'll once again be at peace as I walk on toward my true north.

Thank you for walking with me through these pages, on this road none of us would ever have chosen. May my time spent living this horror movie (with its unexpectedly funny rom-com moments) become a blessing for you.

—Martha

# Bray Family Photos

Our wedding, June 23, 1984

Tory at the Superbowl in New York with the Seahawks and his dad.

Everything baseball.

TRAGEDY TO TRIUMPH · 145

Snowmobiling adventure at Mountain Springs Lodge with part of the Less Talking, More Doing Club. Arleen, Sue and Dave, Michelle and Norm, John and Linda, Kari, John and Carrie, Doug and Sandy, Bob and Martha.

Bob building Legos with Tyler at our kitchen table.

Martha and Bob at the Cystic Fibrosis Foundation auction in Bellevue in 2019.

Celebrating Bob's purchase of Dairy Distributing, 1992.

TRAGEDY TO TRIUMPH · 147

Wedding of Tyler and Stephanie with Bob's parents, Bob and Louise Bray.

Touring Doune Castle in Scotland, site of the filming of *Monty Python and the Holy Grail*.

Bray family photo, 2004.

# A Note from Martha

One of the reasons I believe Heaven is real is that I was there, briefly, when I was four.

It happened on the Fourth of July, 1966. Our whole clan was gathered: Mom, Dad, my sisters Margaret and Marlene, Uncle Bill, Auntie Jan, cousins and more, forty family members in all, at my maternal grandparents' beach house on the southeast shore of Lake Samish south of Bellingham.

A sunny day, puffy, shifting clouds, barely warm enough to swim but we kids don't care: We are whooping, laughing, racing in and out, splashing, building trenches in the muddy sand, floating a plastic toy boat. In shallow water, a pack of cousins in inner tubes link hands, forming a floating, shifting train. The sun sparkles on ripply water, lily pads populate the shallows. Just up the grassy slope of my grandparents' property, Dad mans the backyard grill, tongs in hand; the smell of grilling hamburgers wafts down to us. Mom's at the picnic table on the patio, rummaging in the cooler. Uncle Bill is next to her, chatting, cold pop in hand. Seeing my adults up on the lawn and the kids playing in the water wraps me in happiness. I find an inner tube on shore, grab it, and splash out to join the train of floating cousins.

One cousin in the middle of the train tips, laughs, falls out of the tube, causing chaos as everyone dumps into the shallow water. For a moment, it's bedlam, and I fall underneath what's left of the tangled inner-tube train. I know how to swim but it doesn't matter, because I am face-down in the silt of the lake bottom. I am being trampled by unsuspecting cousins. Silently, hysterically, madly, I try to struggle upward but can't free myself from the churning tangle of kids' arms, legs, trunks, feet.

My consciousness fades. I drown.

I remember feeling peaceful. I remember being in a lovely, tranquil place full of light with an overwhelming sense of peace. I remember wanting to stay there, not wanting to return to the pandemonium of the day that only moments before had held such happiness for me. I want to stay in this beautiful, celestial place.

But Uncle Bill intervenes. Flinging down his bottle of pop, sprinting the few yards to the water, he hauls me out, lays me flat on the picnic table, and starts CPR on my little chest before anyone else knows what's happening. But—I am told later—I remain unresponsive.

Uncle Bill was one of the first CPR instructors in Washington, and after ten minutes of maneuvering, of using every CPR method known to man at the time, I am suddenly back, coughing and spitting water, my lungs gasping for air.

Decades later, as a young mother myself, I ask my mom about her memories of that Fourth of July event. Did she worry I'd be brain-damaged for life?

"Oh honey," Mom said, "we still worry."

# A Note from Cheryl

Though I never met Bob Bray, I learned of him in January 2023 when *Business Pulse* magazine assigned me to write a memorial piece. As I interviewed his friends and associates, my admiration for this unknown man grew.

Thus, I thrilled to meet, across a pickleball net on Labor Day 2024, a fellow player named Martha Bray. Martha, widow of the esteemed Bob Bray! At the potluck supper following pickleball, I nabbed the seat across from her to ask her about life after Bob. As she told stories from heart-wrenching to hilarious, I was moved from tears to laughter to astonishment; Martha's stories covered the range of human emotions.

As we finished our paper plates of potato salad and strawberry-pretzel Jell-O salad, Martha said, "People keep telling me, I ought to write a book."

"I can help you with that," I said.

And here we are. You hold the result in your hands.

## Remembering Bob Bray

By Cheryl Stritzel McCarthy

*Reprinted with permission from Business Pulse magazine*

Bob Bray was such a well-liked and well-respected member of the community, people expected his funeral would be full of tears.

It was the opposite. The Celebration of Life in honor of Bray—like the man himself—was faith-filled and brimming with joyful memories. "It was the most positive memorial I've been to in my life," said longtime friend Tim Trott, retired owner of the former Lee's Drive-In in Bellingham. About 700 people packed Christ the King Community Church on Oct. 13, 2022, for Bray's service.

Many who came wore not funeral black, but crimson and gray, the colors of Bray's beloved Washington State University Cougars. He would've liked that.

As the pastor read tribute after tribute from Bray's legions of friends and business associates—you couldn't do business with Bray without becoming his friend—those who came to mourn felt lifted up.

Before the dreadful September day when a traffic accident took his life, you would not have thought of Bray as a towering figure, as an icon of Whatcom County. He was not flashy or up-front or in the headlines. He was, instead, a behind-the-scenes embodiment of the best of Whatcom County's business community: a beloved husband, father, and grandfather; a business owner who ran Dairy Distributing based on trust; a rock-solid member of Northlake Community Church who volunteered with Young Life and Royal Family Kids camps.

He was also just plain fun. Ed Mack, owner of Cruisin Coffee, said Bray was always joyful at the Royal Family Kids golf tournament. Bray's team, filled with coworkers from Dairy Distributing, including his son Tyler, "was rowdy and full of fun, raising money for those kids," Mack said.

Diane Brainard, owner of Old Town Café on West Holly Street in Bellingham, has known Bray since 1989. "Dairy Distributing is a small company that's run very professionally with a lot of heart. I don't think I ever had a problem with any orders, which is rare in this business.

"Bob's legacy is that he ran a successful business with people he loved," Brainard said. "He put his staff first and that showed with how well the business ran. I know he was trying to retire but couldn't quite let go. Bob was a devout Christian and he showed it every day."

Fahri Ugurlu, former manager of Hotel Bellwether, moved to this area in 1999. As an unknown, other vendors asked him to personally guarantee his hotel's bills, but Bray told Ugurlu's hotel chef to get what he wanted from Dairy Distributing's warehouse and just let him know. "Bob had tremendous trust in his employees and customers," Ugurlu said.

Doug Thomas, president and CEO of Bellingham Cold Storage, said he and his wife Sandy met Bob and Martha Bray about 2006 when the Brays were leading a Young Life group. Thomas said the center of Bray's universe, other than his faith, was his wife and sons and their families.

Trott echoes the theme. "Every time we'd motorcycle ride, he was always so thankful for all of creation," Trott said.

Ugurlu remembers a motorcycle ride with Bray and others to WSU where Bray had them all salute the Cougar flag. "When we would see Bob and ask him 'how are you,' he'd always say, "I'm living the life!"

May that joyful celebration of his life continue.

October 2022

# Bound for Glory
## by Cathy Pauley,
### friend of the Bray family

*Excerpted from Friends of Bob Facebook page, edited for clarity and brevity.*

The Celebration of Life is over, but the memories linger. After the service, after the many letters read, after the slideshow of photos of a life well lived, I see on the display table a stack of baseball cards. Created by a family member as a take-home memory for attendees, the card shows Bob in a baseball uniform, his nickname on the front, a Bible verse on the back.

I pick one up, pause, smile. As I stand at the display table, card in hand, I imagine a scene. In my mind's eye, the scene becomes a video, vivid with color and sound. In my mental movie, I see a ballfield, the bleachers packed with friends, family, colleagues, employees, all clapping and chanting "Bob, Bob, Bob." I see Bob exit the dugout, step to the plate, take a practice swing.

The pitch comes in hot, but Bob connects, the hard smack of the bat sending the ball skyward. The crowd erupts: "Holy smokes! My, oh my! See you *later!* It's outta here!"

Bob drops the bat and begins his home run trot. As he steps on first base, he's surrounded by his siblings and their families, folks who've rooted for him since he was born. As he passes second, he's cheered by his sons, daughters-in-law, and grandchildren. The grands yell, "Run, PapaBob, run!" He approaches third for a high-five and hug from his wife, his other half, his life's partner.

Bob turns and heads for home plate, his smile lighting up the ballfield as the crowd roars. Safe! He's home!

When the game's over, when the fans go home, when the bleachers are empty and the bright lights click off, when the great sadness tries to envelop his family and many friends, they can remember his final run to home.

Bound for glory? He's already there.

Bibliography

# Grief Management Resources

Devine, Megan. *It's OK that You are Not OK: Meeting Grief and Loss in a Culture That Doesn't Understand*. Boulder, Colorado: Sounds True, Inc., 2017.

Dultmeier, Jim and Lori, and Nancy Sprowell Geise. *On Shattered Wings, A Family's Journey from Grief to Hope*. Topeka, Kansas: Life Changing Stories LLC, 2021.

Gray, Stephen, and Chris Radtke, writers and directors. *After Death*. Provo, Utah: Angel Studios, 2023, DVD. An American Christian documentary film.

griefshare.org GriefShare, a ministry of Church Initiative, is a national program, in person or online, offering support groups, videos, and more, including the two-hour class "Surviving the Holidays."

McCreery, Scotty. "Christmas in Heaven," track #6 on music album *Christmas with Scotty McCreery*, Mercury Nashville, 2012.

Sandberg, Sheryl, and Adam Grant. *Option B: Facing Adversity, Building Resilience, and Finding Joy*. New York: Alfred A. Knopf, 2017.

Sturgis, Gary. *Surviving: Finding Your Way from Grief to Healing*. St. Petersburg, Florida: BookLocker, 2020.

*We Are Widow Warriors* private Facebook group.

# Acknowledgments

There are a myriad of people who have walked alongside me during this tumultuous two years while my entire world slowly recalibrated. First, I thank the faithful staff at Dairy Distributing for your heroic efforts in keeping the business operational. Bob would have been so proud of you:

Steve Swanson
Skip Ottway
Ron McPherson
John Inge
Jason McIntosh
Tyler Bray

I would never have made it through the valley of grief without so many beloved friends who helped me over every possible bump in the road:

George Harrington
Dave and Sue Schwab
Steve and Julie Clarke
John and Carrie Carter
Tim and Lori Spink

Tim and Kari Dickerson
Dan and Susan Wood
Matt and Janet Chandik
Mike and Sandi Glick
Tim and Jackie Trott
Jon Hansen
Lisa D'Hondt
Mark and Barb Boyson
Arleen Watkinson
Hans and Nancy Bjerno
Kathy Lathrop
Christy Marx
Kim Bajema
Shelly Beld
Diane Marsh
Bonnie Alm
Donna Hilton
Kari Oswald
Jane Linscott
Dori Rauls
Barb Davison
James and Nikki Stewart
Jane Terpsma
Shelly Colglazier
Lori Huard

Thank you all for your endless kindness, your emotional support, your intelligent and timely business help, and for listening to my "can't make this stuff up" stories.

# About the Authors

**Martha Gallman Bray** is a lifelong resident of Bellingham, Washington. After graduating from Western Washington University with a degree in Secondary Education Home Economics, and a minor in physical education, she taught Home Economics at Mount Baker High School in Deming, Washington, starting in 1985, and later taught third grade at Bellingham Christian School. She then held a variety of part-time jobs while focusing on raising two sports-loving sons. Throughout, she served the family business as wife of the director of The World Headquarters of Dairy Distributing, a role that included delivering homemade breakfast casseroles to the staff every Friday morning for more than a decade.

Martha is involved with local churches, Christ the King and Northlake Community, and is a longtime student of the Bible. She is a dedicated volunteer whose charitable endeavors include hosting a group of women weekly to sew for Days For Girls, an international nonprofit that distributes sustainable products that allow girls to stay in school. Martha loves boating, pickleball, hiking, and e-biking. She divides her time between Bellingham and Arizona.

Of all the jobs she's held, including that of Young Life leader, licensed assistant to realtors, receptionist at a large graphic design firm, and now granny-nanny to two of her four grandchildren, her favorite role was being Bob's wife.

**Cheryl Stritzel McCarthy** and her eight siblings grew up with a paintbrush in their hands and a song in their hearts, working at their family's business of renovating old houses in Ames, Iowa. Her book, *Many Hands Make Light Work: A Memoir* is the rollicking true story of growing up in that family in the '60s and '70s.

Cheryl is a journalist whose work has appeared in *The Wall Street Journal*, the *Los Angeles Times*, and the *Chicago Tribune*, which distributed her articles to newspapers and websites around the country. She freelanced for years as a book critic for *The Plain Dealer* in Cleveland. On assignment for publications, she's traveled to Turkey, Hawaii, and Scotland. She lived in London for seven years, writing for global magazines. She holds an MBA from City University in London and a bachelor's in journalism from Iowa State University.

Today, she ghostwrites, edits, and helps publish memoirs. (See cherylstritzelmccarthy.com)

Cheryl, her husband, and their three daughters have lived in Shaker Heights, Ohio; Toledo, Ohio; and Naperville, Illinois. She now resides with her husband in Bellingham, Washington, and travels frequently to visit grandchildren.

Cheryl and Martha met playing pickleball.